# FAVOURITE Chinese RECIPES

By VIVIAN NG
Photography JOHN-RICHARD TAYE
Styling CHRISTINE SHEPPARD

A J.B. Fairfax Press Publication

# THE AUTHOR

*Raised in Singapore, Vivian Ng now lives with her husband, John-Richard Taye, and their two daughters, Lynn and Belle, in Sydney, Australia.*

*Vivian inherited her love for cooking from her mother who was worried that when they left Singapore they would lose the taste of their 'traditional home food'. She hopes that this book will reassure her mother that she is still cooking those traditional recipes and also show her that they are being enjoyed by many others as well. Vivian's extensive experience includes catering and teaching Chinese cooking. Encouraged by her husband, Vivian has selected her favourite recipes and together they have created a truly authentic Chinese cookbook for the home cook.*

EDITORIAL
Food Editor: Rachel Blackmore
Editors: Kirsten John, Linda Venturoni
Editorial Assistant: Sheridan Packer
Editorial Coordinator: Margaret Kelly

DESIGN AND PRODUCTION:
Managers: Sheridan Carter, Anna Maguire
Layout: Lulu Dougherty
Finished Art: Stephen Joseph
Cover design: Jenny Pace

Published by J.B. Fairfax Press Pty Limited
80-82 McLachlan Avenue
Rushcutters Bay, NSW 2011, Australia
A.C.N. 003 738 430

Formatted by J.B. Fairfax Press Pty Limited
Printed by Toppan Printing Co., Hong Kong

JBFP 327
Includes Index
ISBN 1 86343 178 0

DISTRIBUTION AND SALES
**Australia:** Newsagents Direct Distribution
Ph: (02) 353 9911 Fax: (02) 669 2305
**Sales Enquiries:** J.B. Fairfax Press Pty Limited
Ph: (02) 361 6366 Fax: (02) 360 6262
**United Kingdom:** J.B. Fairfax Press Limited
Ph: (0933) 402330 Fax: (0933) 402234

# ABOUT THIS BOOK

The recipes in this book use fresh chillies, ginger and garlic. These ingredients are available already minced in bottles from supermarkets, and will save you having to crush, chop and mince when time is short. Once opened they keep well in the refrigerator.

Remember when cooking Chinese food much depends on your personal taste and that the quantities of herbs and spices can be varied to suit. Do not be put off making a recipe just because you do not have one of the ingredients, if you check the glossary on page 76 you will probably find a suitable alternative. For those who enjoy and regularly cook Chinese food a trip to an Oriental food store is worth while – you can stock up on special ingredients and you will find that most of the sauces keep very well.

## MICROWAVE OVEN

Where microwave instructions occur in this book a microwave oven with a 650 watt output has been used. Wattage on domestic microwave ovens varies between 500 and 700 watts. It may be necessary to vary the cooking times slightly depending on your oven.

## WHAT'S IN A TABLESPOON?

AUSTRALIA
1 tablespoon = 20 mL or 4 teaspoons
NEW ZEALAND
1 tablespoon = 15 mL or 3 teaspoons
UNITED KINGDOM
1 tablespoon = 15 mL or 3 teaspoons
The recipes in this book were tested in Australia where a 20 mL tablespoon is standard. The tablespoon in the New Zealand and the United Kingdom sets of measuring spoons is 15 mL. For recipes using baking powder, gelatine, bicarbonate of soda, small quantities of flour and cornflour, simply add another teaspoon for each tablespoon specified.

# CONTENTS

# SNACKS

*Serve a selection of these delicious snacks and nibbles for
a special supper. Children especially will love Crispy Spring Rolls
while Curry Puffs and Pork Balls with Chilli Sauce make perfect
party starters with drinks for grown-ups.*

## CURRY PUFFS

Oven temperature
220°C/425°F/Gas 7

1$^1$/2 tablespoons curry powder
1 tablespoon vegetable oil
1 small onion, chopped
90 g/3 oz beef mince or mince of
your choice
1 large potato, diced
$^1$/2 teaspoon salt
$^1$/4 teaspoon sugar
$^3$/4 cup/185 mL/6 fl oz water
375 g/12 oz prepared puff pastry
milk

1   Heat wok or frying pan over a low
heat, add curry powder and cook, stirring,
for 1-2 minutes or until fragrant. Add oil
and onion and cook, stirring, for 4-5
minutes or until onions are soft. Add
beef, potato, salt and sugar and mix to
combine. Stir in water, bring to
simmering and simmer for 20-25 minutes
or until potato is tender and most of the
moisture is absorbed. Remove pan from
heat and set aside to cool completely.

2   Roll pastry out to 5 mm/$^1$/4 in thick
and using a 7.5 cm/3 in fluted cutter cut
out 45 rounds. Place a spoonful of mince
mixture in the centre of each pastry
round. Brush edges lightly with water and
fold pastry over filling. Press edges
together to seal. Place puffs on lightly
greased baking trays, brush each with a
little milk and bake for 10-15 minutes or
until pastry is puffed and golden.

*Makes 45*

The filling should be
completely cold before
making the curry puffs. If
possible make it the day
before and refrigerate
overnight. If the filling is hot or
warm, it will cause the fat in
the pastry to run and the
cooked pastry will be tough
and soggy.
A slice of hard-boiled egg
placed on top of the filling
before folding and sealing
the pastry makes a delicious
variation.
Curry Puffs freeze well and
can be reheated in the oven
from frozen for 20 minutes or
until heated through.

*Crispy Spring Rolls, Curry Puffs*

# CRISPY SPRING ROLLS

50 spring roll wrappers, each
12.5 cm/5 in square
1 egg white, lightly beaten
vegetable oil for deep-frying

MEAT AND VEGETABLE FILLING
4 dried Chinese mushrooms
salt
$1/4$ teaspoon sugar
$1/4$ teaspoon freshly ground black pepper
$1/2$ teaspoon light soy sauce
$1/2$ teaspoon sesame oil
1 teaspoon cornflour
185 g/6 oz chicken or pork mince
1 carrot, grated
375 g/12 oz cabbage, shredded
3 cloves garlic, finely chopped
2 tablespoons oyster sauce

1   To make filling, place mushrooms in a bowl, cover with boiling water and set aside to soak for 10 minutes or until mushrooms are tender. Drain, remove stalks if necessary and cut mushrooms into thin strips.

2   Place $1/4$ teaspoon salt, sugar, black pepper, soy sauce, sesame oil and cornflour in a bowl and mix to combine. Add chicken or pork and mushrooms, toss to combine and set aside to marinate for 10-15 minutes.

3   Place carrot and cabbage in a saucepan and sprinkle with a little salt, cover and cook over a medium heat, tossing occasionally, for 4-5 minutes or until cabbage starts to wilt. Add mince mixture, garlic and oyster sauce and cook, tossing occasionally, for 4-5 minutes longer or until mince changes colour. Drain off liquid and set aside to cool completely.

4   Place a tablespoon of filling in the centre of each wrapper, fold one corner over filling, then tuck in sides and roll up, sealing with egg white.

5   Heat vegetable oil in a wok or large saucepan until a cube of bread dropped in browns in 50 seconds and cook a few spring rolls at a time for 3-4 minutes or until golden. Drain on absorbent kitchen paper and serve immediately.

*Makes 50*

Rest the cooled prepared meat filling in the refrigerator for 3 hours or overnight. It will be much firmer and easier to work with.

*Prawn and Pork Toast*

# PRAWN AND PORK TOAST

4 medium uncooked prawns, shelled
and deveined, finely chopped
125 g/4 oz pork mince
1 small onion, finely chopped
³/4 teaspoon salt
¹/4 teaspoon freshly ground black pepper
¹/4 teaspoon sesame oil
4 slices wholemeal bread, crusts
trimmed
2 tablespoons sesame seeds
vegetable oil for deep-frying
chilli sauce

*Makes 16*

1   Place prawns, pork, onion, salt, black pepper and sesame oil in a bowl and mix to combine. Set aside to marinate for 10-15 minutes.

2   Spread each bread slice with pork mixture and sprinkle with sesame seeds. Cut each slice into 4 triangles.

3   Heat vegetable oil in a wok or large saucepan until a cube of bread dropped in browns in 50 seconds. Cook triangles mince side down, a few at a time, for 4-5 minutes or until golden and cooked through. Remove and drain on absorbent kitchen paper. Serve immediately with chilli sauce for dipping.

Chicken mince can be used
in place of pork if you wish.

# PORK BALLS WITH CHILLI SAUCE

This is an excellent party starter. Serve pork balls on a platter with small bowls of the dipping sauce and plum sauce for those guests who prefer to dip into something less spicy.

1 clove garlic, minced
$^1/_2$ teaspoon salt
$^1/_2$ teaspoon sugar
$^1/_2$ teaspoon freshly ground black pepper
1 teaspoon cornflour
185 g/6 oz pork mince
1 tablespoon vegetable oil
$^1/_4$ cup/30 g/1 oz dried breadcrumbs
vegetable oil for deep-frying
440 g/14 oz pineapple pieces, drained
3 spring onions, cut into 5 cm/2 in pieces

CHILLI DIPPING SAUCE
$^1/_3$ cup/90 mL/3 fl oz chilli sauce
2 tablespoons tomato sauce
1 teaspoon sugar
$^1/_2$ teaspoon salt
$^1/_2$ teaspoon sesame oil
2 teaspoons sesame seeds

1  Place garlic, salt, sugar, black pepper and cornflour in a bowl and mix to combine. Add pork, toss to combine and set aside to marinate for 10-15 minutes.

2  To make dipping sauce, place chilli sauce, tomato sauce, sugar, salt, sesame oil and sesame seeds in a small bowl and mix to combine. Set aside.

3  Stir 1 tablespoon vegetable oil into pork mixture and mix to combine. Roll pork mixture into walnut-sized balls. Place a few pork balls at a time with the breadcrumbs in a plastic food bag and shake to coat balls with crumbs.

4  Heat vegetable oil in a wok or large saucepan until a cube of bread dropped in browns in 50 seconds, and cook pork balls, a few at a time, for 7-10 minutes or until golden and cooked through. Remove pork balls and drain on absorbent kitchen paper. Spear each pork ball with a toothpick or cocktail stick and serve with pineapple pieces, spring onions and dipping sauce.

*Makes 12*

*Pork Balls with Chilli Sauce*

# SAVOURY PANCAKES

### PANCAKES
1 cup/125 g/4 oz flour
1/4 teaspoon salt
pinch sugar
1 cup/250 mL/8 fl oz water
1 egg
1 teaspoon vegetable oil

### MEAT AND VEGETABLE FILLING
3 dried Chinese mushrooms, diced
1 tablespoon vegetable oil
1 small onion, diced
125 g/4 oz mince of your choice
1 small carrot, diced
1 teaspoon light soy sauce
1/2 teaspoon salt
1/2 teaspoon sesame oil
1/2 teaspoon sugar
pinch freshly ground black pepper
2 large potatoes, cooked and mashed
2 tablespoons chopped fresh coriander

1   To make pancakes, place flour, salt and sugar in bowl and mix to combine. Whisk in water, egg, and vegetable oil and continue to whisk until smooth.

2   Heat a lightly greased wok or frying pan over a high heat, pour 2 tablespoons batter into pan and swirl pan so batter covers base thinly and evenly. Cook for 1-2 minutes or until bubbles form on the surface, then turn and cook for 1-2 minutes longer or until pancake is golden. Remove pancake from pan, set aside and keep warm. Repeat with remaining batter to use all the batter.

3   To make filling, place mushrooms in a bowl, cover with boiling water and set aside to soak for 10 minutes or until mushrooms are tender. Drain, remove stalks if necessary and dice mushrooms.

4   Heat vegetable oil in a wok or frying pan over a medium heat, add onion and stir-fry for 2-3 minutes or until onion is transparent. Add mince and stir-fry for 2-3 minutes longer or until it changes colour. Stir in carrot, mushrooms, soy sauce, salt, sesame oil, sugar and black pepper and cook for 4-5 minutes longer or until carrot is soft. Add mashed potato and coriander and mix to combine. Remove pan from heat and set aside to cool.

5   Divide mince mixture between pancakes and place in the centre of each one, fold in sides and roll up. Serve hot or warm.

*Makes 8*

This dish can be made ahead of time and reheated in the microwave on HIGH (100%) for 2 minutes.

*Savoury Pancakes*

# CHINESE PORK BUNS

20 x 5 cm/2 in square pieces nonstick
baking paper

BARBECUED PORK FILLING
1 tablespoon vegetable oil
185 g/6 oz Chinese barbecued pork or
Chinese roast pork, diced
1 clove garlic, crushed
1 tablespoon oyster sauce
1 teaspoon light soy sauce
$^{1}/_{2}$ teaspoon sesame oil
$^{3}/_{4}$ teaspoon sugar
$^{1}/_{4}$ teaspoon salt
$^{1}/_{4}$ teaspoon freshly ground black pepper
1 tablespoon cornflour blended with
5 tablespoons water
2 tablespoons chopped fresh coriander

BUN DOUGH
2 cups/250 g/8 oz self-raising flour
1 tablespoon baking powder
$^{1}/_{3}$ cup/90 g/3 oz sugar
$^{3}/_{4}$ cup/185 mL/6 fl oz water

For a whiter dough, use milk
in place of the water and
add $^{1}/_{2}$ teaspoon of white
vinegar.
Chinese barbecued pork
or Chinese roast pork is
available from Oriental food
stores where it may be
known as char siew.

1  To make filling, heat vegetable oil in
a wok or frying pan over a medium heat,
add pork and garlic and stir-fry for 2-3
minutes or until fragrant. Stir in oyster
sauce, soy sauce, sesame oil, sugar, salt,
black pepper and cornflour mixture and
bring to simmering. Simmer for 3-4
minutes or until mixture is quite dry.
Remove pan from heat, stir in coriander
and set aside to cool completely.

2  To make dough, sift flour and baking
powder together into a large bowl. Add
sugar and mix to combine. Mix in water
to form a soft dough. Turn dough onto a
lightly floured surface and knead for 10
minutes or until dough is smooth. Cover
and set aside to rest for 30 minutes.

3  Divide dough into 20 portions and
working on a lightly floured surface, roll
each portion into a ball. Lightly flatten
each ball of dough to make a 7.5 cm/3 in
round. Place a teaspoon of filling in the
centre of each dough round. Draw pastry
around mixture and pinch together
to form a bun.

4  Place bun join side up on a piece of
the baking paper and place in a bamboo
steamer. Repeat with remaining dough
rounds to use all ingredients.

5  Cover steamer with lid, place over a
saucepan of simmering water and steam
for 10-15 minutes or until buns are
cooked through.

*Makes 20*

*Chinese Pork Buns, Garlic Pork Rolls*

# GARLIC PORK ROLLS

1 kg/2 lb lean pork mince
350 g/11 oz canned water chestnuts,
finely chopped
1 small onion, finely chopped
1 head garlic, cloves separated and
crushed
2 egg whites, lightly beaten
$^1/_3$ cup/90 mL/3 fl oz vegetable oil
5 teaspoons raw (muscovado) or
demerara sugar
$3^1/_2$ teaspoons five spice powder
$1^1/_2$ teaspoons ground coriander
1 teaspoon salt
$^1/_2$ teaspoon freshly ground black pepper
2 teaspoons sesame oil
2 teaspoons light soy sauce
100 g/$3^1/_2$ oz dried bean curd sheets
vegetable oil for deep-frying

*Makes 20*

1   Place pork, water chestnuts, onion, garlic, half egg white mixture, vegetable oil, sugar, five spice powder, coriander, salt, black pepper, sesame oil and soy sauce, in a bowl and mix to combine.

2   Cut bean curd sheet according to fold lines and wipe with a damp cloth. Place pork mixture along centre of bean curd sheets, fold in sides and roll up. Brush edges with remaining egg white and seal, cover and refrigerate overnight.

3   Heat vegetable oil in a wok or large saucepan until a cube of bread dropped in browns in 50 seconds, and cook rolls in batches, turning occasionally, for 5-10 minutes or until golden and cooked through. Remove rolls from pan and drain on absorbent kitchen paper. Slice and serve immediately.

Dried bean curd sheets are available from Oriental food stores and some health food shops and supermarkets. This is the skin that forms during the making of bean curd. It is skimmed off the boiled mixture, then dried. It is also called bean curd skin.
Serve with a salad of sliced cucumber, sliced tomatoes and pineapple pieces and accompany with chilli sauce for dipping.

# SOUPS

*Traditionally the Chinese serve soup at the end of a banquet but these light and tasty soups can be eaten at any time. What could be nicer than a steaming bowl of Creamy Corn and Crab Soup or Garlic Pork Spare Rib Soup to warm up a winter's day?*

## GARLIC PORK SPARE RIB SOUP

1.5 kg/3 lb pork spare ribs, separated
6 cups/1.5 litres/2$^1$/$_2$ pt water
1 tablespoon heavy soy sauce
(kicap soya)
$^1$/$_3$ cup/90 mL/3 fl oz light soy sauce
4 tablespoons raw (muscovado) or
demerara sugar
$^1$/$_2$ teaspoon salt
300 g/9$^1$/$_2$ oz Chinese fried bread sticks
(yau-char-kwai), sliced (optional)
2 tablespoons chopped fresh coriander
2 red chillies, seeded and finely chopped

SPICE BAG
10-12 cloves garlic, lightly bruised
4 whole cloves
2 star anise
1 tablespoon whole white or black
peppercorns, lightly crushed
1 piece muslin, 20 cm/8 in square

1   Place ribs in a large saucepan and pour over enough hot water to cover. Bring to the boil over a medium heat and boil for 4-5 minutes. Remove from heat, drain ribs and rinse under cold running water to remove scum. Discard cooking water.

2   To make Spice Bag, place garlic, cloves, star anise and white or black peppercorns in the centre of the piece of muslin. Draw up corners and tie securely.

3   Place water and Spice Bag in a large saucepan and bring to the boil. Add parboiled spare ribs, heavy soy sauce (kicap soya), light soy sauce, sugar and salt, reduce heat and simmer for 2$^1$/$_2$ -3 hours or until ribs are tender. Garnish with bread slices, if using. Sprinkle with coriander and serve with chillies.

*Serves 4*

Chinese fried bread sticks (yau-char-kwai) are available from Oriental food stores.
Heavy soy sauce labelled as kicap soya has a thick treacle-like consistency and is used more for colour than flavour. It is available from Oriental food stores. If unavailable gravy browning is the perfect substitute.

*Fresh Corn and Pork Soup,*
*Garlic Pork Spare Rib Soup*

# SEAFOOD AND TOFU SOUP

10 uncooked medium prawns, shelled
and deveined, tails left intact
125 g/4 oz squid (calamari), cleaned
$^1/_2$ teaspoon salt
$^1/_2$ teaspoon sugar
$^1/_2$ teaspoon cornflour
$^1/_4$ teaspoon freshly ground black pepper
$^1/_4$ teaspoon sesame oil
water
185 g/6 oz firm white fish fillet, sliced
1 tablespoon vegetable oil
3-5 thin slices fresh ginger
300 g/9$^1/_2$ oz block tofu, halved
lengthwise and sliced
1 small carrot, sliced
2 teaspoons chicken stock powder
2-3 spring onions, cut into
2.5cm/1 in lengths

1   Cut prawns in half lengthwise. Make a single cut down the length of each squid (calamari) tube or body and open out. Using a sharp knife, cut parallel lines down the length of the squid (calamari), taking care not to cut right through the flesh. Make more cuts in the opposite direction to form a diamond pattern. Cut each piece into 3 or 4 pieces.

2   Place salt, sugar, cornflour, black pepper, sesame oil and 1 tablespoon water in a bowl and mix to combine. Add prawns, squid (calamari) and fish, toss to combine and set aside to marinate for 10-15 minutes.

3   Heat vegetable oil in a wok or large saucepan, add ginger and stir-fry for 2-3 minutes or until fragrant. Stir in 3 cups/ 750 mL/1$^1/_4$ pt water and bring to the boil. Add seafood mixture, tofu, carrot and chicken stock powder and cook for 5 minutes or until seafood is cooked. Remove pan from heat, sprinkle with spring onions and serve immediately.

*Serves 4*

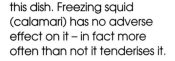

Either fresh or frozen squid (calamari) can be used for this dish. Freezing squid (calamari) has no adverse effect on it – in fact more often than not it tenderises it.

# FRESH CORN AND PORK SOUP

This soup is also easy to make in the microwave. Place water, corn and pork in a microwave-safe dish and cook on HIGH (100%) for 8-10 minutes. Then cook on MEDIUM (50 %) for 1 hour or until pork is tender and soup is a light yellow colour. Season to taste.

2.2 litres/3$^3/_4$ pt water
6 cobs fresh corn, each cut into 3 pieces
750 g/1$^1/_2$ lb lean pork, cubed
$^1/_2$ teaspoon raw (muscovado) or
demerara sugar
salt
freshly ground white pepper

Place water in a saucepan and bring to the boil. Add corn pieces, pork and sugar and boil for 15 minutes, then reduce heat and simmer for 2 hours or until soup is a light yellow colour. Season to taste with salt and white pepper and serve.

*Serves 4*

*Seafood and Tofu Soup*

# TOMATO AND EGG THREAD SOUP

1 tablespoon light soy sauce
$^1/_2$ teaspoon cornflour
2 tablespoons vegetable oil
$^1/_2$ teaspoon sesame oil
$^1/_4$ teaspoon sugar
$^1/_4$ teaspoon salt
125 g/4 oz lean pork mince
2 cups/500 mL/16 fl oz water
2 cloves garlic, lightly bruised
1 large tomato, cut into wedges
2 eggs, lightly beaten with
$^1/_2$ teaspoon salt and $^1/_4$ teaspoon sugar
1 tablespoon chopped fresh coriander

To achieve perfect 'threads' in soups and stocks it is important to switch the heat off, before adding the beaten egg mixture. If the eggs are added to soup while the heat is still on, lumpy and firm blobs will result rather than delicate threads.

1  Place soy sauce, cornflour, 3 teaspoons vegetable oil, sesame oil, sugar and salt in a bowl and mix to combine. Add pork, toss to combine and set aside to marinate for 10-15 minutes.

2  Place water, garlic and remaining vegetable oil in a saucepan and bring to the boil. Stir in pork mixture, bring to simmering and simmer for 3-5 minutes or until pork is cooked. Add tomato and simmer for 1 minute longer. Switch off heat and immediately stir egg mixture into soup – use a fork and circular motion so that the egg mixture forms thin threads in the soup. Sprinkle with coriander and serve immediately.

*Serves 2*

# CREAMY CORN AND CRAB SOUP

Left: Tomato and Egg Thread Soup
Above: Creamy Corn and Crab Soup

440 g/14 oz canned creamed corn
1³/4 cup/440 mL/14 fl oz water
185 g/6 oz crabmeat
1¹/2 teaspoons cornflour blended with
1 tablespoon water
1 egg, lightly beaten
1 teaspoon vinegar
¹/4 teaspoon sugar
freshly ground black pepper

Place corn and water in a saucepan and bring to the boil over a medium heat. Stir in crabmeat and cornflour mixture and bring to simmering. Remove from heat, stir in egg, vinegar and sugar and season to taste with black pepper. Serve immediately.

*Serves 4*

For something different make this soup using pork mince instead of the crabmeat.

# FISH AND SEAFOOD

*To the Chinese, serving fish or seafood is a sign of prosperity. At a formal banquet, the hosts always serve whole fish with the head pointing towards the guest of honour to assure him or her of good fortune.*

## STIR-FRIED SQUID

500 g/1 lb squid (calamari), cleaned
4 tablespoons vegetable oil
8 cloves garlic, sliced
8 fresh red chillies, sliced
5 cm/2 in piece fresh ginger, sliced
1 onion, sliced
$1^1/4$ teaspoons cornflour blended with
4 tablespoons water
2 teaspoons light soy sauce
1 teaspoon lemon juice
1 teaspoon salt
$^1/2$ teaspoon sugar
1 teaspoon sesame oil
3 spring onions, cut into
3 cm/$1^1/4$ in lengths

To clean squid (calamari), pull tentacles from the squid (calamari), carefully taking with them the stomach and ink bag. Cut the beak, stomach and ink bag from the tentacles and discard. Wash tentacles well. Wash tube (body) and peel away skin. Cut tube into rings or honeycomb and use as desired.

1   Using a sharp knife cut down the length of each squid (calamari) tube or body and lay out flat. Cut parallel lines down the length of squid (calamari), taking care not to cut right through the flesh. Make more cuts in the opposite direction to form a diamond pattern. Cut each piece into 3 or 4 pieces.

2   Heat vegetable oil in wok or frying pan over a high heat, add garlic, chillies, ginger, onion and squid (calamari) pieces and stir-fry for 1-2 minutes or until squid (calamari) is opaque. Add cornflour mixture, soy sauce, lemon juice, salt, sugar, sesame oil and spring onions and stir-fry for 1-2 minutes longer. Serve immediately.

*Serves 4*

*Stir-fried Squid, Stuffed Baby Squid*

# STUFFED BABY SQUID

16 baby squid (calamari) tubes, cleaned
1 tablespoon vegetable oil
60 g/2 oz canned corn kernels, drained
60 g/2 oz fresh or frozen peas
$1/4$ teaspoon salt
2 fresh red chillies, seeded and sliced
2 tablespoons chopped fresh coriander
freshly ground black pepper

### PORK AND MUSHROOM FILLING
4 dried Chinese mushrooms
1 teaspoon light soy sauce
$1/2$ teaspoon cornflour
$1/2$ teaspoon sesame oil
$1/4$ teaspoon salt
$1/4$ teaspoon sugar
$1/4$ teaspoon freshly ground black pepper
125 g/4 oz pork mince
2 tablespoons grated carrot

### GARLIC AND OYSTER SAUCE
1 teaspoon cornflour
$1/2$ teaspoon sugar
$1/2$ teaspoon salt
2 teaspoons oyster sauce
4 tablespoons water
2 cloves garlic, crushed

1  To make filling, place mushrooms in a bowl, cover with boiling water and set aside to soak for 10 minutes or until mushrooms are tender. Drain, remove stalks if necessary and cut mushrooms in half.

2  Place soy sauce, cornflour, sesame oil, salt, sugar and black pepper in a bowl and mix to combine. Add pork, carrot and mushrooms, toss to combine and set aside to marinate for 10-15 minutes.

3  To make sauce, place cornflour, sugar, salt, oyster sauce, water and garlic in a small bowl and mix to combine. Set aside.

4  Rinse squid (calamari) under cold running water and pat dry with absorbent kitchen paper. Three-quarters fill each squid (calamari) tube with filling and secure opening with a wooden toothpick or cocktail stick.

5  Heat vegetable oil in wok or frying pan over a medium heat, add squid (calamari) tubes and stir-fry for 5-6 minutes or until filling expands. Add corn kernels, peas and salt to pan and stir-fry for 3-4 minutes longer. Add sauce, bring to simmering and remove pan from heat. Sprinkle with chillies, coriander and black pepper to taste and serve immediately.

*Serves 4*

Squid (calamari) should always be cleaned before storing. It will keep in the refrigerator for up to 3 days or can be frozen for up to 3 months.
The squid (calamari) tubes used in this recipe should be 5-6 cm/2-2$1/2$ in long.

*Prawns Steamed with Ginger*

# Prawns Steamed with Ginger

1 teaspoon salt
1 teaspoon sugar
$1^1/_2$ teaspoons Chinese rice wine
$1^1/_2$ teaspoons ginger juice
$^1/_2$ teaspoon sesame oil
4 tablespoons vegetable oil
$^3/_4$ teaspoon freshly ground black pepper
16 medium uncooked prawns, washed, shells left intact
1 spring onion, cut into 5 cm/2 in lengths
2 fresh red chillies, seeded and sliced lengthwise

1   Place salt, sugar, wine, ginger juice, sesame oil, vegetable oil and black pepper in a bowl and mix to combine. Add prawns, toss to coat and marinate for 10-15 minutes.

2   Place spring onion in a heatproof bowl, top with prawn mixture and cover with aluminium foil. Place bowl on a wire rack or upturned saucer in a large saucepan and add enough boiling water to come halfway up the sides of the bowl. Cover pan and cook for 7 minutes. Remove pan from heat and stand for 2 minutes. Sprinkle prawns with chillies and serve immediately.

*Serves 4*

To make ginger juice refer to glossary (page 78).
Do not lift the lid during the steaming process or much of the flavour will be lost.
In this recipe the prawns are cooked in their shells.

# ASSAM FISH

2 tablespoons vegetable oil
1 stalk fresh lemon grass, cut into three
or 1 teaspoon dried lemon grass, soaked
in hot water until soft
3 tablespoons tamarind paste dissolved
in $^1/_2$ cup/125 mL/4 fl oz water, strained
$1^1/_2$ cups/375 mL/12 fl oz water
750 g/$1^1/_2$ lb boneless fish fillets
10 okra, sliced diagonally
$1^1/_4$ teaspoons raw (muscovado) or
demerara sugar
1 teaspoon salt
1 teaspoon light soy sauce
1 large tomato, cut into wedges

### REMPAH
1 large onion, coarsely chopped
2 cloves garlic, coarsely chopped
3-5 fresh red chillies, coarsely chopped
2.5 cm/2 in piece fresh ginger, coarsely
chopped
2-4 dried red chillies, soaked in hot
water until soft

Tamarind is available from Indian food shops. It is available as a paste which is dissolved in water then strained before using. If it is unavailable use a mixture of lime or lemon juice and treacle as a substitute. Use 1 part molasses to 3 parts lime or lemon juice to make required quantity, eg 1 tablespoon molasses to 3 tablespoons lime or lemon juice.

1   To make Rempah, place onion, garlic, fresh chillies, ginger and dried chillies in a food processor or blender and process to make a smooth paste. Set aside.

2   Heat oil in wok or saucepan over a medium heat, add Rempah and cook, stirring constantly, for 2-3 minutes or until fragrant. Add lemon grass and tamarind liquid and cook for 5 minutes or until oil begins to separate from paste. Stir in water, bring to simmering and simmer for 15-20 minutes or until mixture thickens.

3   Add fish and okra to pan, cover and cook for 5 minutes or until fish flakes when tested with a fork and okra is tender. Stir in sugar, salt and soy sauce. Top with tomato and serve immediately.

*Serves 4*

# Hot and Tangy Prawns

$^1$/2 teaspoon salt
$^1$/2 teaspoon sugar
$^1$/4 teaspoon freshly ground black pepper
20 medium uncooked prawns, shelled
and deveined, tails left intact
2 tablespoons vegetable oil
6 thin slices fresh ginger
4 cloves garlic, thinly sliced
3 fresh red chillies, sliced
2 spring onions, cut into 5 cm/2 in
lengths
1 tomato, cut into wedges
1 onion, cut into wedges
1 lettuce, leaves separated

TOMATO CHILLI SAUCE
$^3$/4 cup/185 mL/6 fl oz tomato ketchup
or sauce
1$^1$/2 tablespoons chilli sauce
1 teaspoon sugar
$^1$/2 teaspoon salt
1$^1$/2 teaspoons light soy sauce

1   Place salt, sugar and black pepper in a bowl and mix to combine. Add prawns, toss to coat and set aside to marinate for 10-15 minutes.

2   To make sauce, place tomato ketchup or sauce, chilli sauce, sugar, salt and soy sauce in a bowl and mix to combine. Set aside.

3   Heat vegetable oil in wok or frying pan over a medium heat, add ginger, garlic, chillies, spring onions and prawn mixture and stir-fry for 3-4 minutes or until prawns change colour.

4   Add sauce to pan and stir-fry for 1-2 minutes or until heated through. Add tomato and onion and stir-fry for 2-3 minutes longer. Line a serving platter with lettuce leaves, top with prawn mixture and serve immediately.

*Serves 4*

If you prefer a thinner sauce, stir 1-2 tablespoons of water into the pan in step 4. Uncooked prawns should have a firm body and a pleasant sea smell. Discard any prawns which are dark coloured or suspect.

*Left: Assam Fish*
*Right: Hot and Tangy Prawns*

23

# CLAMS IN BLACK BEAN SAUCE

To clean clams, scrub shells well under cold running water. Place clams in a bucket of clean saltwater and leave for 2-3 hours. If leaving longer change the water or the clams will die because of lack of oxygen. Prawns or mussels are also delicious cooked in this way.

2 tablespoons vegetable oil
5 fresh red chillies, chopped finely
4 cloves garlic, chopped finely
1 kg/2 lb clams in shells, cleaned

BLACK BEAN SAUCE
1 1/2 tablespoons black bean garlic sauce
3/4 teaspoon raw (muscovado) or demerara sugar
1/2 teaspoon cornflour
1/4 teaspoon sesame oil
pinch salt
2 teaspoons water

1   To make sauce, place bean sauce, sugar, cornflour, sesame oil, salt and water in a bowl and mix to combine. Set aside.

2   Heat vegetable oil in wok or frying pan over a medium heat, add chillies and garlic and stir-fry 1-2 minutes or until fragrant. Add clams and cook, stirring, for 4-5 minutes or until shells open. Discard any clams that do not open after 5 minutes cooking. Stir in sauce and cook for 1-2 minutes longer.

*Serves 4*

# STIR-FRIED FISH AND VEGETABLES

When buying frozen fish watch out for freezer burn; this indicates that the fish has been wrapped incorrectly before freezing and has dehydrated. Freezer burn appears as dry, white or brown patches on the flesh of the frozen fish.

350 g/11 oz boneless fish fillets
1/2 teaspoon salt
1/2 teaspoon cornflour
1/4 teaspoon sugar
1/4 teaspoon freshly ground black pepper
1/2 teaspoon water
2 1/2 tablespoons vegetable oil
6-8 thin slices fresh ginger
5 cobs canned baby sweet corn, drained and cut in half lengthwise then crosswise
1/2 carrot, sliced
2 spring onions, cut into 2.5 cm/1 in lengths

SHERRY SAUCE
3/4 cup/185 mL/6 fl oz water
3/4 teaspoon cornflour
1 1/4 teaspoons salt
1/2 teaspoon raw (muscovado) or demerara sugar
1/2 teaspoon sesame oil
1/2 teaspoon light soy sauce
1/2 teaspoon sweet sherry

*Serves 4*

1   Pat fish fillets dry with absorbent kitchen paper and set aside. Place salt, cornflour, sugar, black pepper and water in a bowl and mix to combine. Add fish fillets, toss to coat and set aside to marinate for 10-15 minutes.

2   To make sauce, combine water, cornflour, salt, sugar, sesame oil, soy sauce and sherry in a bowl. Set aside.

3   Heat 2 tablespoons vegetable oil in wok or frying pan over a medium heat, add ginger and stir-fry for 1-2 minutes or until fragrant. Add fish fillets and stir-fry for 2-3 minutes or until almost cooked, add sweet corn and carrot, and stir-fry for 1-2 minutes longer. Remove fish and vegetables from pan and set aside.

4   Heat remaining vegetable oil in pan, add sauce mixture and bring to simmering, stirring constantly. Return fish and vegetables to pan, add spring onions and stir-fry for 1-2 minutes longer.

*Clams in Black Bean Sauce,*
*Stir-fried Fish and Vegetables*

# STIR-FRIED FISH AND BROCCOLI

315 g/10 oz boneless fish fillets, cut
into large pieces
salt
freshly ground black pepper
cornflour
3 tablespoons vegetable oil
1 small head broccoli, cut into small
florets
2 cloves garlic, thinly sliced
1 small onion, cut into wedges
1 small tomato, cut into wedges
$^1/_2$ cup/125 mL/4 fl oz water
1 tablespoon light soy sauce
$^1/_4$ teaspoon sesame oil

This recipe is also delicious
made using chicken. Use
chicken breast fillets, cut into
cubes and cook for 4-5
minutes or until just cooked in
step 2.

1   Season fish fillets with $^1/_2$ teaspoon
salt and black pepper to taste and toss in
2 tablespoons cornflour.

2   Heat vegetable oil in a wok or frying
pan over a medium heat, add fish and

cook, turning frequently, until golden on
both sides and flesh flakes when tested
with a fork. Remove fish from pan, set
aside and keep warm.

3   Add broccoli, garlic and $^1/_4$ teaspoon
salt to pan and stir-fry for 3-4 minutes or
until broccoli just changes colour. Add
onion and tomato to pan and stir-fry for
2-3 minutes longer. Spoon vegetable
mixture over fish and set aside.

4   Combine water, soy sauce,
$^1/_2$ teaspoon salt, $^1/_2$ teaspoon cornflour
and sesame oil in a small bowl and mix to
combine. Stir cornflour mixture into pan
and cook, stirring, for 1-2 minutes or until
sauce boils and thickens slightly. Spoon
sauce over fish and vegetables and serve.

*Serves 4*

# CHILLI CRABS

2 uncooked crabs, cleaned and cut into quarters
vegetable oil for deep-frying
1 tomato, cut into wedges
1 egg, lightly beaten
<sup>1</sup>/2 lettuce, leaves separated

### CHILLI AND ONION PASTE
2 onions, roughly chopped
5 cm/2 in piece fresh ginger, roughly chopped
4 fresh red chillies, roughly chopped
5 cloves garlic, halved
2 tablespoons water

### PEANUT AND TOMATO SAUCE
$^1/_3$ cup/90 mL/3 fl oz tomato sauce
2 tablespoons peanut butter
1 tablespoon cornflour
$^3/_4$ cup/185 mL/6 fl oz water
1 teaspoon dried shrimp powder
1 teaspoon salt
3 teaspoons raw (muscovado) or demerara sugar
2 teaspoons light soy sauce

1   Lightly smash crab claws with cleaver and set aside.

2   To make paste, place onions, ginger, chillies, garlic and water in a food processor or blender and process to make a smooth paste. Set aside.

3   To make sauce, place tomato sauce, peanut butter, cornflour, water, shrimp powder, salt, sugar and soy sauce in a bowl and mix to combine. Set aside.

4   Heat vegetable oil in a wok or large saucepan until a cube of bread dropped in browns in 50 seconds and cook crabs in batches for 3-4 minutes or until they just change colour. Remove crabs and drain on absorbent kitchen paper. Drain all but 2 tablespoons of oil from pan.

5   Heat reserved oil in wok or saucepan, add onion paste and stir-fry for 2-3 minutes or until fragrant. Add crabs and peanut sauce, bring to simmering and simmer for 4-5 minutes or until sauce just begins to thicken. Stir in tomato. Remove pan from heat and stir in egg. Line a large serving platter with lettuce leaves, top with crab mixture and serve immediately.

*Serves 4*

The sweetest crab meat is always the most difficult to get to. Rinse sticky fingers in finger bowls of warm water with a squeeze of lemon juice.

*Left: Stir-fried Fish and Broccoli*
*Right: Chilli Crabs*

# BEEF

*The popular Chinese stir-fry is colourful, economical and everyone's favourite. As it is one of the quickest methods of cooking, it's important to have all your ingredients ready before you begin. Marinades, both sweet and spicy, add distinctive flavour to these beef recipes.*

## MEATBALL CURRY

2 tablespoons curry powder
2 tablespoons vegetable oil
$^3/_4$ cup/185 mL/6 fl oz water
$^1/_2$ cup/125 mL/4 fl oz coconut milk
1 teaspoon salt
$^3/_4$ teaspoon sugar
1 small eggplant (aubergine), quartered lengthwise and cut crosswise into wedges
1 tomato, cut into wedges

GINGERED BEEF BALLS
250 g/8 oz beef mince
$^1/_4$ onion, diced
1 teaspoon curry powder
$^1/_2$ teaspoon ground ginger
$^1/_2$ teaspoon sugar
$^1/_4$ teaspoon salt
1 tablespoon vegetable oil

GINGER PASTE
$^1/_4$ onion, chopped
1 thin slice fresh ginger
2 cloves garlic, chopped
1 teaspoon water

1  To make beef balls, place beef, onion, curry powder, ginger, sugar and salt in a bowl, mix to combine and set aside to marinate for 15 minutes. Stir oil into meat mixture. Roll spoonfuls of meat mixture into balls and set aside.

2  To make paste, place onion, ginger, garlic and water in a food processor or blender and process to make a smooth paste. Set aside.

3  Heat a wok or frying pan over a medium heat, add curry powder and cook, stirring, for 2-3 minutes. Remove curry powder from pan and set aside. Add oil to pan and heat. Add Ginger Paste and stir-fry for 2-3 minutes or until fragrant. Stir curry powder, water, coconut milk, salt and sugar into pan, bring to simmering and simmer over a low heat for 8-10 minutes or until mixture thickens slightly.

4  Add beef balls and eggplant (aubergine) to curry mixture. Cover pan, bring to simmering, and simmer for 15-20 minutes or until beef balls are cooked. Just prior to serving, add tomato and mix to combine.

*Serves 4*

Serve this tasty curry on a bed of boiled rice or noodles accompanied by mango chutney.
To prevent eggplant (aubergine) from discolouring, place in lightly salted water, drain well and pat dry on absorbent kitchen paper before adding to pan.

*Meatball Curry, Beef and Pepper Stir-fry*

# SATAY BEEF

1 teaspoon curry powder
1 teaspoon ground cumin
$^1/_2$ teaspoon ground anise
$^1/_2$ teaspoon saffron powder
$^1/_2$ teaspoon salt
2 teaspoons light soy sauce
2 teaspoons raw (muscovado) or
demerara sugar
4 tablespoons vegetable oil
500 g/1 lb topside beef, cut into
3 cm/1$^1/_4$ in wide strips
1 cucumber, sliced
1 onion, sliced

SATAY SAUCE
100 g/3$^1/_2$ oz roasted peanuts
1 small onion, chopped
3 cloves garlic, chopped
2 teaspoons shrimp powder
1 teaspoon chilli powder
$^1/_3$ cup/90 mL/3 fl oz peanut
(groundnut) oil
3 teaspoons raw (muscovado) or
demerara sugar
$^1/_3$ cup/90 mL/3 fl oz coconut milk
1 cup/250 mL/8 fl oz water
1 small tomato, diced

Coconut milk can be
purchased in a number of
forms: canned, as a long-life
product in cartons, or as a
powder to which you add
water. Once opened it has a
short life and should be used
within a day or so. It is
available from Oriental food
stores and most supermarkets.

1   Place curry powder, cumin, anise, saffron, salt, soy sauce and sugar in a bowl and mix to combine. Stir in vegetable oil and beef, toss to combine and set aside to marinate for 10-15 minutes.

2   To make sauce, place peanuts, onion and garlic in a food processor or blender and process to finely chop. Add shrimp powder and chilli powder and process to combine.

3   Heat peanut (groundnut) oil in a saucepan over a medium heat, reduce heat to low, add peanut mixture and cook, stirring, for 8-10 minutes or until fragrant – take care not to burn the mixture. Stir in sugar and coconut milk and bring to simmering, stirring constantly, over a low heat. Stir in water and bring to the boil. Add tomato and mix to combine.

4   Thread meat strips onto lightly oiled skewers and cook under a preheated hot grill or on a barbecue for 2-3 minutes each side or until meat is tender. Serve with sliced cucumber, sliced onion and Satay Sauce.

*Makes 30*

*Satay Beef*

# BEEF AND PEPPER STIR-FRY

$^3/_4$ teaspoon sugar
$^1/_2$ teaspoon salt
$^1/_4$ teaspoon freshly ground black pepper
$^1/_2$ teaspoon sesame oil
$^1/_2$ teaspoon vinegar
500 g/1 lb topside beef, cut into thin strips
1 tablespoon vegetable oil
2.5 cm/1 in piece fresh ginger, thinly sliced
3 cloves garlic, crushed
1 red pepper, sliced
1 green pepper, sliced
6 mushrooms, sliced

### OYSTER SAUCE
$^1/_2$ teaspoon cornflour
1 tablespoon water
3 teaspoons oyster sauce
1 teaspoon sweet sherry
$^1/_4$ teaspoon salt

1   Place sugar, salt, black pepper, sesame oil and vinegar in a bowl and mix to combine. Add beef, toss to combine and set aside to marinate for 10-15 minutes.

2   To make sauce, place cornflour, water, oyster sauce, sherry and salt in a bowl and mix to combine. Set aside.

3   Heat vegetable oil in a wok or frying pan over a medium heat, add ginger and garlic and stir-fry for 2-3 minutes or until fragrant. Add beef mixture and stir-fry for 3-4 minutes or until almost cooked. Add red pepper, green pepper and mushrooms and stir-fry for 2-3 minutes longer. Push all ingredients to side of pan, add sauce and cook, stirring, for 1 minute or until mixture boils. Push meat mixture into sauce and stir-fry for 1 minute longer.

*Serves 4*

Sesame oil is used as a flavouring, but not usually for cooking. It has a strong distinctive flavour and only a small quantity is required. It is available from Oriental food stores and most supermarkets and keeps indefinitely.

# CLAY POT BEEF

1 teaspoon freshly ground black pepper
$^1/_2$ teaspoon cornflour
$^1/_4$ teaspoon sugar
$^1/_4$ teaspoon salt
2 tablespoons water
500 g/1 lb topside beef, sliced diagonally
2 tablespoons vegetable oil
3 thin slices fresh ginger
2 cloves garlic, thinly sliced
$^1/_2$ carrot, sliced diagonally
60 g/2 oz straw mushrooms, halved
60 g/2 oz canned bamboo shoots, sliced
60 g/2 oz snow peas (mangetout)

SHERRY SAUCE
2 tablespoons water
1 tablespoon oyster sauce
1 tablespoon semi-sweet sherry
1 tablespoon light soy sauce
$^1/_2$ teaspoon cornflour
$^1/_2$ teaspoon sugar
$^1/_4$ teaspoon salt

1   Place black pepper, cornflour, sugar, salt and water in a bowl and mix to combine. Add beef, toss to combine and set aside to marinate for 10-15 minutes.

2   To make sauce, place water, oyster sauce, sherry, soy sauce, cornflour, sugar and salt in a bowl and mix to combine. Set aside.

3   Place oil and ginger in a clay pot or casserole dish and heat over a medium heat for 2-3 minutes or until hot. Add garlic and beef mixture and stir-fry over a high heat for 4-5 minutes or until almost cooked. Add carrot, mushrooms, bamboo shoots, snow peas (mangetout) and Sherry Sauce, mix to combine and cover. Turn off heat and leave for 1-2 minutes.

*Serves 4*

Soy sauce is an essential ingredient in Asian cooking. The Chinese use two types of soy sauce – light soy sauce, labelled as Superior Soy, and dark soy sauce, labelled as Soy Superior Sauce. Generally, Western cooks prefer to use the light soy sauce – it is not as strong.

# STIR-FRIED BEEF AND BABY CORN

¹/₄ teaspoon salt
¹/₄ teaspoon sugar
¹/₄ teaspoon freshly ground black pepper
2 teaspoons water
1¹/₂ teaspoons light soy sauce
¹/₂ teaspoon sesame oil
1 teaspoon cornflour
¹/₂ teaspoon bicarbonate of soda
3 tablespoons vegetable oil
125 g/4 oz topside beef, cut into thin strips
220 g/7 oz canned straw mushrooms, sliced
2 carrots, cut into 5 cm/2 in strips
315 g/10 oz canned baby sweet corn, drained and sliced
1 large onion, sliced
125 g/4 oz green beans, cut into 5 cm/2 in pieces
3 spring onions, cut into 5 cm/2 in lengths
4 cloves garlic, thinly sliced
1 tablespoon dry sherry

SESAME AND SOY SAUCE
¹/₂ teaspoon cornflour
¹/₂ teaspoon salt
¹/₄ teaspoon sugar
¹/₃ cup/90 mL/3 fl oz water
¹/₂ teaspoon light soy sauce
¹/₄ teaspoon sesame oil

1  Place salt, sugar, black pepper, water, soy sauce, sesame oil, cornflour, bicarbonate of soda and 1 teaspoon vegetable oil in a bowl and mix to combine. Add beef, toss to combine and set aside to marinate for 10-15 minutes.

2  To make sauce, place cornflour, salt, sugar, water, soy sauce and sesame oil in a small bowl and mix to combine. Set aside.

3  Heat remaining vegetable oil in a wok or frying pan over a high heat, add beef mixture and stir-fry for 2-3 minutes or until beef just changes colour. Remove beef from pan and set aside. Add mushrooms, carrots, sweet corn, onion, beans, spring onions and garlic and stir-fry for 3-4 minutes or until vegetables are almost cooked. Return beef to pan, add sauce and stir-fry for 2-3 minutes longer or until heated through. Stir in sherry and serve immediately.

*Serves 4*

There are two types of wok available: the Cantonese wok and the pau wok. The Cantonese wok has a handle on either side while the pau has just one long handle. The Cantonese wok is better for steaming and deep-frying, while the pau wok is best for stir-frying.

*Left: Clay Pot Beef*
*Right: Stir-fried Beef and Baby Corn*

# STEAMED BEEF OMELETTE

2 teaspoons light soy sauce
$1/4$ teaspoon sesame oil
$1/4$ teaspoon vegetable oil
pinch sugar
pinch freshly ground black pepper
155 g/5 oz beef mince
3 eggs
$1/4$ teaspoon salt
1 cup/250 mL/8 fl oz water
1 teaspoon ginger oil (optional)
1 spring onion, finely chopped
1 fresh red chilli, finely chopped

Accompany with boiled rice
or noodles.
This recipe is also delicious
made using pork mince
instead of beef.
To make ginger oil refer to
glossary (page 78).

1   Place 1 teaspoon soy sauce, sesame oil, vegetable oil, sugar and black pepper in a bowl and mix to combine. Add beef, toss to combine and set aside to marinate for 10-15 minutes.

2   Place eggs and salt in a bowl and whisk to combine. Stir in water and mince mixture and mix well. Pour egg mixture into a lightly oiled small ovenproof dish. Place dish on a rack over simmering water in a large saucepan, cover and steam over a low heat for 8-10 minutes or until set. Sprinkle with ginger oil, if using, and remaining soy sauce and garnish with spring onion and chilli.

*Serves 4*

*Left: Steamed Beef Omelette*
*Above: Spicy Mince Stir-fry*

# SPICY MINCE STIR-FRY

1¹/₂ tablespoons vegetable oil
1 onion, chopped
2 fresh red chillies, chopped
1 clove garlic, chopped
500 g/1 lb lean beef mince
2 mushrooms, chopped
125 g/4 oz fresh or frozen peas
1¹/₂ tablespoons light soy sauce
1¹/₂ tablespoons Worcestershire sauce
1 teaspoon cornflour blended with
1 tablespoon water
¹/₂ teaspoon sweet soy sauce
(kechap manis)
1 teaspoon sugar
³/₄ teaspoon salt
¹/₄ teaspoon freshly ground black pepper
1 tablespoon chopped fresh coriander

Heat oil in a wok or frying pan over a high heat, add onion and chillies and stir-fry for 2-3 minutes or until fragrant. Add garlic, beef, mushrooms, peas, light soy sauce, Worcestershire sauce, cornflour mixture, sweet soy sauce (kechap manis), sugar, salt and black pepper and stir-fry for 5 minutes or until mixture is almost dry. Remove pan from heat, stir in coriander and serve immediately.

*Serves 4*

This mixture is delicious served in lettuce cups. Spoon the mixture into the lettuce leaves, roll up and eat.
If sweet soy sauce (kechap manis) is unavailable a mixture of soy sauce and golden syrup can be used in its place.

# PORK

*Whether it's barbecued, sweet and sour or steamed, pork is one of the most popular meats in Chinese cooking. There's something for everyone amongst these recipes which include Pork and Bamboo Curry and Crispy Saffron Pork.*

## SWEET AND SOUR PORK

$^{1}/_{2}$ teaspoon salt
$^{1}/_{2}$ teaspoon sugar
$^{1}/_{4}$ teaspoon freshly ground pepper
$^{3}/_{4}$ teaspoon light soy sauce
1 egg yolk
375 g/12 oz diced lean pork
$^{1}/_{4}$ cup/30 g/1 oz cornflour
vegetable oil for deep-frying

SWEET AND SOUR SAUCE
1 tablespoon vegetable oil
$^{1}/_{2}$ cup/125 mL/4 fl oz water
3 tablespoons sugar
$^{1}/_{4}$ teaspoon salt
$2^{1}/_{2}$ tablespoons tomato sauce
2 teaspoons chilli sauce
2 teaspoons Worcestershire sauce
2 teaspoons white vinegar
$^{1}/_{2}$ teaspoon sesame oil
1 tablespoon cornflour blended with
$2^{1}/_{2}$ tablespoons water
1 onion, cut into eighths and separated
1 tomato, cut into eighths
1 cucumber, cut into chunks
125 g/4 oz pineapple pieces
2 fresh red chillies or $^{1}/_{2}$ red pepper,
seeded and finely chopped

1  Place salt, sugar, black pepper, soy sauce and egg yolk in a bowl and whisk to combine. Add pork and toss to coat. Place cornflour in a plastic food bag. Drain pork, add to bag with cornflour and toss to coat. Shake off excess cornflour.

2  Heat vegetable oil in a wok or large saucepan until a cube of bread dropped in browns in 50 seconds, and cook pork in batches for 5 minutes or until golden and cooked. Remove and drain on absorbent kitchen paper. Set aside and keep warm.

3  To make sauce, heat vegetable oil in a wok or saucepan, stir in water, sugar, salt, tomato sauce, chilli sauce, Worcestershire sauce, vinegar and sesame oil and stirring constantly, bring to simmering. Add cornflour mixture and cook, stirring constantly, for 3-4 minutes or until sauce boils and thickens. Add onion, tomato, cucumber, pineapple and chillies or red pepper and cook, stirring, for 1 minute. Add pork and cook for 1-2 minutes longer or until heated through. Serve immediately.

*Serves 4*

One of the most popular and undoubtedly famous Chinese recipes, Sweet and Sour Pork is delicious served with steamed or boiled rice and steamed Chinese cabbage.

*Pork Balls in Tomato Sauce,
Sweet and Sour Pork*

# Pork Balls in Tomato Sauce

1 1/2 tablespoons light soy sauce
1 teaspoon cornflour
1/2 teaspoon sugar
1/2 teaspoon sesame oil
1/4 teaspoon salt
1/4 teaspoon freshly ground black pepper
250 g/8 oz lean pork mince
3 tablespoons vegetable oil
2 potatoes, halved and sliced
1/2 carrot, halved and sliced
1 onion, halved and sliced
30 g/1 oz fresh or frozen peas
2 cloves garlic, sliced
1 tablespoon chopped fresh coriander

TOMATO SAUCE
1/2 cup/125 mL/4 fl oz tomato ketchup
or sauce
1/2 cup/125 mL/4 fl oz water
2 teaspoons sugar
1/2 teaspoon salt
1/2 teaspoon light soy sauce

1  Place soy sauce, cornflour, sugar, sesame oil, salt and black pepper in a bowl and mix well to combine. Add pork, toss to combine and set aside to marinate for 10-15 minutes. Take dessertspoons of pork mixture and roll into balls.

2  To make sauce, place tomato ketchup or sauce, water, sugar, salt and soy sauce in a bowl and mix to combine.

3  Heat 1 tablespoon vegetable oil in a wok or frying pan over a medium heat and stir-fry potatoes for 4-5 minutes or until golden and tender. Remove potatoes from pan and set aside.

4  Heat 1 tablespoon vegetable oil in pan over a high heat, add pork balls a few at a time and cook for 3-4 minutes or until cooked through. Remove pork balls from pan and set aside.

5  Heat remaining vegetable oil in pan over a medium heat, add carrot, onion, peas and garlic and stir-fry for 1 minute.

6  Stir Tomato Sauce into pan and cook for 1 minute. Return potatoes and pork balls to pan and cook, stirring constantly, for 3-4 minutes or until heated through. Sprinkle with coriander and serve immediately.

*Serves 4*

Lean beef mince can be used in place of the pork if you wish.

*Pork Ribs in Oyster Sauce*

# Pork Ribs in Oyster Sauce

1 1/2 tablespoons oyster sauce
2 cloves garlic, crushed
1/4 teaspoon sugar
1/2 teaspoon chilli powder
1 1/2 teaspoons sweet soy sauce
(kechap manis)
500 g/1 lb pork spare ribs, separated
vegetable oil for deep-frying
2 tablespoons water

*Serves 4*

1   Place oyster sauce, garlic, sugar, chilli powder and sweet soy sauce (kechap manis) in a bowl and mix well to combine. Add ribs and set aside to marinate for 1 hour. Drain and reserve marinade.

2   Heat oil in a wok or large saucepan until a cube of bread dropped in browns in 50 seconds, and cook ribs in batches for 4-5 minutes or until golden and crispy. Remove ribs, drain on absorbent kitchen paper, set aside and keep warm.

3   Drain pan of all but 2 teaspoons oil, add reserved marinade and water and cook, stirring, for 3-4 minutes or until sauce begins to simmer. Serve as a dipping sauce with ribs.

# CRISPY SAFFRON PORK

1 egg, beaten
3 tablespoons light soy sauce
1 1/2 teaspoons sugar
1/2 teaspoon salt
1 teaspoon chilli powder
1 teaspoon vinegar
1/2 teaspoon saffron powder
500 g/1 lb belly pork, skin removed, sliced
2 tablespoons vegetable oil
1/4 lettuce, shredded

1   Place egg, 2 tablespoons soy sauce, sugar, salt, chilli powder, vinegar and saffron in a bowl and whisk to combine. Add pork, toss to combine and set aside to marinate for 10-15 minutes.

2   Heat oil in a wok over a high heat, add pork mixture and stir-fry for 7-10 minutes or until golden and cooked through. Switch off heat and stir in remaining soy sauce. Line a serving platter with lettuce, top with pork mixture and serve immediately.

*Serves 4*

When planning a Chinese or Asian-style meal, try to choose dishes that use a variety of cooking methods and ingredients. In this way you will have not only a combination of textures and flavours but you will also find cooking and serving easier.

# MARINATED PORK CHOPS

1 tablespoon oyster sauce
1 tablespoon sweet soy sauce
(kechap manis)
1 teaspoon hoisin sauce
1/2 teaspoon sugar
1/2 teaspoon freshly ground black pepper
1/2 teaspoon salt
1/4 teaspoon vinegar
6 lean pork chops
2 tablespoons vegetable oil
1 large onion, sliced

1   Place oyster sauce, sweet soy sauce (kechap manis), hoisin sauce, sugar, black pepper, 1/4 teaspoon salt and vinegar in a bowl and mix to combine. Pierce chops several times with a fork to tenderise. Place in a shallow glass or ceramic dish, pour over sauce mixture, turn to coat chops well and set aside to marinate for 15-30 minutes.

2   Heat 1 tablespoon oil in a frying pan over a medium heat, add onion and remaining salt and stir-fry for 3-4 minutes or until onion is golden. Remove onion mixture from pan and set aside.

3   Heat remaining oil in frying pan, add chops and cook for 4-5 minutes each side or until tender. Serve chops garnished with fried onions.

*Serves 4*

If sweet soy sauce (kechap manis) is unavailable use a mixture of 3 1/2 tablespoons soy sauce and 1/2 teaspoon golden syrup.

*Crsipy Saffron Pork, Marinated Pork Chops*

# BEAN SPROUTS AND PORK STIR-FRY

4 dried Chinese mushrooms
1 teaspoon oyster sauce
sugar
1 teaspoon light soy sauce
salt
$^1/_4$ teaspoon sesame oil
pinch freshly ground black pepper
185 g/6 oz lean pork, cut into thin strips
2 tablespoons vegetable oil
2.5 cm/1 in piece fresh ginger, cut into
thin strips
250 g/8 oz bean sprouts
2 spring onions, cut into 5 cm/2 in strips
$^1/_2$ red pepper, cut into thin strips
2 cloves garlic, sliced
$^1/_2$ teaspoon cornflour blended with
1$^1/_2$ tablespoons water and $^1/_4$ teaspoon
sesame oil

1   Place mushrooms in a bowl, cover
with boiling water and set aside to soak
for 10 minutes or until mushrooms are
tender. Drain and remove stalks if
necessary and cut mushrooms into strips.
Place mushrooms in a small bowl, add
oyster sauce and $^1/_4$ teaspoon sugar, toss
to coat and set aside.

2   Place soy sauce, $^1/_4$ teaspoon salt,
sesame oil, pinch sugar and black pepper
in a bowl and mix to combine. Add pork,
toss to combine and set aside to marinate
for 10-15 minutes.

3   Heat 1 tablespoon vegetable oil in a
wok or frying pan over a medium heat,
add pork mixture, mushrooms and ginger
and stir-fry for 2-3 minutes or until pork
changes colour. Remove pork mixture
from pan and set aside. Heat remaining
vegetable oil in pan over a medium heat,
add bean sprouts, spring onions, red
pepper, garlic and salt to taste and stir-fry
for 1 minute. Return pork mixture to pan
and stir in cornflour mixture. Cook,
stirring, for 1 minute or until mixture
thickens slightly and is heated through.

*Serves 4*

*Left: Bean Sprouts and Pork Stir-fry*
*Right: Pork in Bean Sauce*

# Pork in Bean Sauce

500 g/1 lb pork belly, sliced or cubed
1¹/₂ teaspoons sugar
2 tablespoons vegetable oil
3 cloves garlic, bruised
1¹/₂ tablespoons yellow bean sauce
1¹/₂ tablespoons heavy soy sauce
(kicap soya)
1 teaspoon chilli paste (sambal oelek)
¹/₂ teaspoon salt
fresh red chillies, chopped (optional)

*Serves 4*

1   Place pork in a bowl, add 1 teaspoon sugar, toss to combine and set aside to marinate for 10-15 minutes.

2   Heat oil in a wok or frying pan over a medium heat, add garlic and bean sauce and stir-fry for 1-2 minutes or until fragrant. Add pork mixture to pan and stir-fry for 4-5 minutes or until pork is brown. Stir in heavy soy sauce (kicap soya), chilli paste (sambal oelek), remaining sugar and salt, bring to simmering and simmer, stirring occasionally, for 10 minutes or until pork is tender. Sprinkle with chillies, if using.

Yellow bean sauce is a thick, spicy sauce made from yellow beans, flour and salt. It has a distinctive flavour and is available from Oriental food stores. There are two varieties: whole yellow bean sauce or crushed yellow bean sauce. The whole yellow bean sauce is less salty and has a better texture.

# PORK AND BAMBOO SHOOTS

1 teaspoon cornflour
1$^1$/$_2$ teaspoons sugar
2 teaspoons light soy sauce
1 tablespoon shrimp powder (optional)
500 g/1 lb lean pork, cut into thin strips
1 tablespoon vegetable oil
1 onion, finely chopped
2 cloves garlic, crushed
1 teaspoon finely grated fresh ginger
1$^1$/$_2$ teaspoons chilli powder or 2 fresh
red chillies, chopped
1$^1$/$_2$ teaspoons salt
$^1$/$_4$ teaspoon saffron powder
1$^1$/$_2$ cups/375 mL/12 fl oz coconut milk
220 g/7 oz canned bamboo shoots, cut
into strips

1  Place cornflour, $^1$/$_2$ teaspoon sugar,
1$^1$/$_2$ teaspoons soy sauce and shrimp
powder, if using, in a bowl and mix to
combine. Add pork, toss to combine and
set aside to marinate for 10-15 minutes.

2  Heat oil in a wok or large frying pan,
add onion, garlic, ginger, chilli powder or
chillies and salt and stir-fry for 2-3
minutes or until fragrant. Add saffron
and coconut milk and stirring constantly,
bring mixture slowly to simmering.

3  Add pork mixture and bamboo shoots
to pan and simmer for 10-15 minutes or
until meat is tender and cooked through.
Stir in remaining sugar and remaining soy
sauce and serve immediately.

*Serves 4*

To avoid lumpy or foamy
results when cooking with
coconut milk or cream: only
simmer on a low heat. Never
boil and never cover.

# SPICY STIR-FRIED PORK

2 cloves garlic, crushed
4 tablespoons light soy sauce
3$^1$/$_2$ tablespoons vegetable oil
1 teaspoon sesame oil
1 teaspoon sugar
1 teaspoon salt
1 teaspoon freshly ground black pepper
500 g/1 lb pork fillet, sliced
$^1$/$_4$ lettuce, shredded
fresh red chillies, chopped (optional)
Chinese plum sauce

1  Place garlic, soy sauce, 2 teaspoons
vegetable oil, sesame oil, sugar, salt and
black pepper in a bowl and mix well to
combine. Add pork, toss to combine and
set aside to marinate for 10-15 minutes.

2  Heat remaining vegetable oil in a wok
or frying pan over a high heat. Add pork
and stir-fry for 7-10 minutes or until
golden and cooked through. Drain oil
from pan and dry-fry pork until crispy on
the edges. Line a serving platter with
lettuce, top with pork mixture and
sprinkle with chillies, if using. Serve with
plum sauce.

*Serves 4*

Plum sauce is available from
Oriental food stores and most
supermarkets. Made from
dried plums, apricots,
vinegar, sugar and spices,
it is a thick, sweet chutney-
like sauce that is used as a
condiment.

*Pork and Bamboo Shoots, Spicy Stir-fried Pork*

# CHICKEN AND DUCK

*The choice and variety of poultry dishes available in Chinese cooking is endless. Both ducks and chickens are highly regarded and no banquet is complete without them. Some of the best are presented here, including Paper-wrapped Chicken, Spicy Fried Duck and Braised Chicken with Chestnuts.*

## TANGY LEMON CHICKEN

3¹/₂ tablespoons vegetable oil
1 kg/2 lb chicken pieces, cut into
bite-sized pieces
10 cm/4 in piece fresh lemon grass from
base of stem, bruised or ¹/₂ teaspoon
dried lemon grass, soaked in hot water
until soft
¹/₂ cup/125 mL/4 fl oz water
¹/₄ cup/60 mL/2 fl oz fresh lemon or
lime juice
3 teaspoons sugar
2 teaspoons salt

REMPAH
5 dried red chillies, seeded and chopped
3 fresh red chillies, seeded
1 clove garlic
2 onions, roughly chopped
1 candlenut or macadamia nut

1   To make Rempah, place dried chillies in a bowl, pour over enough boiling water to cover and set aside to stand for 10 minutes or until soft. Drain well. Place soaked chillies, fresh chillies, garlic, onions and candlenut or macadamia nut in a food processor or blender and process to make a smooth paste.

2   Heat oil in a wok or frying pan over a medium heat, add Rempah and cook, stirring frequently, for 4-5 minutes or until paste darkens. Add chicken pieces and lemon grass and stir-fry for 5 minutes or until chicken is golden. Reduce heat to low and cook, adding water gradually and stirring frequently, for 10 minutes longer or until chicken is cooked.

3   Stir in lemon or lime juice, sugar and salt and bring to the boil. As soon as the mixture boils, remove from heat and serve.

*Serves 4*

*Tangy Lime Chicken, Crispy Chicken Wings*

It is important not to overcook the chicken or the meat will break down and the flavour of the lemon or lime will change.

# CRISPY CHICKEN WINGS

1$^1$/2 teaspoons salt
1 teaspoon light soy sauce
$^1$/2 teaspoon sugar
1 teaspoon Chinese rice wine
16 large chicken wings, cut at joints
vegetable oil for deep-frying

1   Place salt, soy sauce, sugar and wine in a bowl and mix to combine. Add chicken, toss to coat and set aside to marinate for 10-15 minutes.

2   Heat oil in a wok or large saucepan until a cube of bread dropped in browns in 50 seconds and cook chicken wings for 5 minutes or until golden, crisp and cooked through.

*Serves 4*

Serve with small dishes of five spice powder, salt and pepper for dipping.

# BRAISED CHICKEN WITH CHESTNUTS

75 g/2$^1$/2 oz dried chestnuts
2 tablespoons vegetable oil
500 g/1 lb boneless chicken breast
fillets, cut into bite-sized pieces
1 cm/$^1$/2 in piece fresh ginger
1 tablespoon heavy soy sauce
(kicap soya)
1 tablespoon light soy sauce
2 teaspoons salt
1$^3$/4 teaspoons sugar
$^1$/2 teaspoon sesame oil
1$^1$/4 cup/315 mL/10 fl oz water

1   Place chestnuts in a bowl and pour over enough hot water to cover. Set aside to soak for 30 minutes or until chestnuts are soft. Using the tip of a small sharp knife, carefully remove skin from chestnuts, drain well and set aside.

2   Heat vegetable oil in a wok or frying pan over a high heat, add chicken and ginger and stir-fry for 3-4 minutes or until chicken changes colour. Stir chestnuts, heavy soy sauce (kicap soya), light soy sauce, salt, sugar, sesame oil and water into pan, cover and bring to simmering. Reduce heat to low and simmer, stirring occasionally, for 30 minutes or until chicken and chestnuts are tender.

*Serves 4*

If the mixture seems too dry add a little more water during cooking.
For more information on heavy soy sauce see glossary (page 78).

*Braised Chicken with Chestnuts*

# PAPER-WRAPPED CHICKEN

2 tablespoons Chinese rice wine
2 tablespoons oyster sauce
1 tablespoon light soy sauce
1 teaspoon sugar
1 teaspoon ginger juice
$^1/_2$ teaspoon freshly ground black pepper
$^1/_2$ teaspoon sesame oil
$^1/_4$ teaspoon salt
1 kg/2 lb chicken wings, cut at joints
baking paper
cornflour paste
vegetable oil for deep-frying

1   Place wine, oyster sauce, soy sauce, sugar, ginger juice, black pepper, sesame oil and salt in a bowl and mix to combine. Add chicken wings, toss to coat and set aside to marinate for 10-15 minutes.

2   Cut and fold four pieces of baking paper into envelopes as shown and seal edges of envelopes with cornflour paste. Divide chicken wings between envelopes and seal tops with cornflour paste.

3   Heat vegetable oil in a wok or large saucepan until a cube of bread dropped in browns in 50 seconds. Cook, one or two envelopes at a time, for 5 minutes or until chicken is cooked. Remove envelopes from oil and drain on absorbent kitchen paper. Remove chicken from wrappers and serve immediately.

*Serves 4*

To make cornflour paste, place $^1/_2$ cup/60 g/2 oz cornflour in a bowl and mix in sufficent water to make a thick smooth paste.
In Asia a wok would usually be used for deep-frying, however it is probably easier and safer to use a deep-fat fryer or a deep-sided saucepan.
To make ginger juice refer to glossary (page 78).

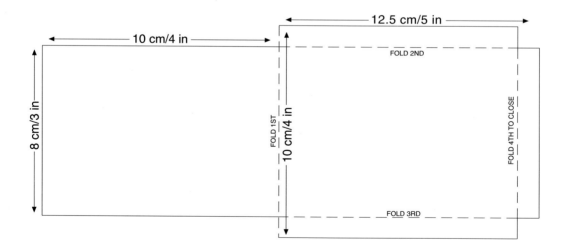

*Paper-wrapped Chicken*

# DUCK WITH BLACK BEAN SAUCE

Oven temperature
180°C, 350°F, Gas 4

2 kg/4 lb duck
$^1/_3$ cup/90 mL/3 fl oz Chinese
plum sauce
$^1/_2$ teaspoon salt
1 cucumber, sliced

BLACK BEAN SAUCE
2 teaspoons sugar
2 teaspoons black bean garlic sauce
1 teaspoon sesame oil
8 tablespoons Chinese plum sauce
1 fresh red chilli, cut into thin strips

1   Cut duck down back and lay out flat.
Wash and pat dry with absorbent kitchen
paper. Place plum sauce and salt in a
small bowl and mix to combine. Rub
plum sauce mixture over duck and set
aside to marinate for 30 minutes.

2   Place duck in a baking dish and bake
for 1 hour or until cooked.

3   To make sauce, place sugar, bean
sauce, sesame oil, plum sauce and chilli in
a small bowl and mix to combine.

4   To serve, cut duck into pieces and
accompany with cucumber and sauce.

*Serves 4*

This dish looks great served
on a bed of sliced cucumber
and garnished with shredded
ginger and fresh coriander.

52

# FRAGRANT STEAMED CHICKEN

*Left: Duck with Black Bean Sauce*
*Above: Fragrant Steamed Chicken*

3 dried Chinese mushrooms, stalks removed
1 tablespoon cloud ear fungi
$^1/_4$ cup/60 mL/2 fl oz oyster sauce
$^1/_4$ cup/60 mL/2 fl oz vegetable oil
1 tablespoon water
1 teaspoon light soy sauce
$^3/_4$ teaspoon sugar
$^1/_2$ teaspoon salt
$^1/_4$ teaspoon freshly ground black pepper
$^3/_4$ teaspoon sesame oil
4 boneless chicken breast fillets, sliced
8 thin slices fresh ginger
2 fresh red chillies, seeded and cut into thin strips
2 tablespoons shredded spring onions

1 Place dried mushrooms and fungi in separate bowls, pour over enough boiling water to cover and set aside to stand for 10 minutes or until tender. Drain, rinse under cold running water and cut into thin strips.

2 Place oyster sauce, vegetable oil, water, soy sauce, sugar, salt, black pepper and sesame oil in a bowl and mix to combine. Add chicken, mushrooms and fungi and mix to combine. Place chicken mixture on a lightly oiled heatproof plate, sprinkle with ginger and chillies and set aside to marinate for 10 minutes.

3 Place plate of prepared chicken mixture in a bamboo steamer set over a saucepan of simmering water, cover and steam for 10 minutes or until chicken is cooked. Alternatively, cover with microwave plastic wrap and cook on HIGH (100%) for 4 minutes. Sprinkle with spring onions and serve immediately.

*Serves 4*

Cloud ears, also known as wood ears, are black fungi available from Oriental food stores. Like dried Chinese mushrooms they have to be soaked in hot water until they are tender before using. If they are unavailable use two extra dried mushrooms.

# CHICKEN IN RED BEAN CURD

$^3/_4$ cube red bean curd
$^1/_2$ teaspoon sugar
$^1/_2$ teaspoon salt
1 teaspoon chilli powder
1 kg/2 lb chicken wings, cut at joints
2 tablespoons cornflour
vegetable oil for deep-frying

1   Place red bean curd, sugar, salt and chilli powder in a bowl and mash to combine. Add chicken, toss to coat and set aside to marinate for 15-30 minutes.

2   Place chicken and cornflour in a plastic food bag, shake to coat chicken with cornflour. Shake off excess cornflour.

3   Heat oil in wok or large saucepan until a cube of bread dropped in browns in 50 seconds.  Deep-fry chicken in batches for 5 minutes or until golden and crisp and cooked through. Remove from pan, drain on absorbent kitchen paper and serve immediately.

*Serves 6*

Red bean curd is available from Oriental food stores. It is pressed bean curd which has been fermented with rice wine, salt, spices and red rice. It has a pungent flavour and is available in jars or cans.

# STIR-FRIED SESAME CHICKEN

$^1/_3$ cup/90 mL/3 fl oz water
1 teaspoon cornflour
1 teaspoon dark soy sauce
2 tablespoons sesame oil
$^3/_4$ teaspoon salt
$^3/_4$ teaspoon sugar
500 g/1 lb boneless chicken breast fillets, cut into 5 cm/2 in strips
2 tablespoons vegetable oil
5 cm/2 in piece fresh ginger, cut into thin strips
1 teaspoon Chinese rice wine
1 tablespoon sesame seeds, toasted
3 spring onions, cut into 5 cm/2 in lengths

1   Place 1 tablespoon water, cornflour, soy sauce, 1 teapoon sesame oil, salt and sugar in a bowl and mix to combine. Add chicken, toss to coat and set aside to marinate for 10-15 minutes.

2   Heat vegetable oil in a wok or frying pan over a medium heat, add ginger and stir-fry for 2-3 minutes or until fragrant and crispy. Add chicken mixture and stir-fry for 3-4 minutes or until chicken changes colour. Stir in remaining water, remaining sesame oil and wine and stir-fry for 3-4 minutes longer or until chicken is cooked through. Sprinkle with sesame seeds and spring onions and serve immediately.

*Serves 4*

The easiest way to toast a small quantity of sesame seeds is to place the seeds in a small frying pan and heat over a medium heat. Shake the pan frequently, until seeds pop and are golden. Take care not to burn the seeds.

*Chicken in Red Bean Curd, Stir-fried Sesame Chicken*

*Above: Spicy Fried Duck*
*Right: Chicken in Oyster Sauce*

# SPICY FRIED DUCK

1¹/₂ teaspoons salt
1 teaspoon five spice powder
2 kg/4 lb duck, cleaned
vegetable oil for deep-frying
1 cucumber, sliced
dipping sauce of your choice

1  Combine salt and five spice powder and set aside.

2  Holding duck by neck, ladle hot water over body, then drain well and pat dry with absorbent kitchen paper. Rub five spice mixture over skin of duck. Hang duck in an airy place for 3-4 hours.

3  Heat oil in a wok or large saucepan until a cube of bread dropped in browns in 50 seconds. Add duck and cook for 10-15 minutes or until crisp and golden and cooked through. Remove duck from oil and drain on absorbent kitchen paper.

4  To serve, cut duck into pieces and accompany with cucumber and dipping sauce.

*Serves 4*

Five spice powder is a favourite ingredient in Chinese cooking. It adds a subtle anise flavour to Oriental dishes.

# CHICKEN IN OYSTER SAUCE

2¹/₂ tablespoons vegetable oil
500 g/1 lb chicken pieces, chopped into
bite-sized pieces
4 fresh green chillies, cut into
1 cm/¹/₂ in pieces
3 thin slices fresh ginger
¹/₃ cup/90 mL/3 fl oz oyster sauce
1 teaspoon dark soy sauce
¹/₂ teaspoon sugar
¹/₂ teaspoon salt
2 cloves garlic, sliced
2 spring onions, sliced diagonally
2 tablespoons chopped fresh coriander

1   Heat oil in a wok or frying pan over a
high heat. Add chicken, chillies and
ginger and stir-fry for 3-4 minutes or until
chicken is golden.

2   Stir in oyster sauce, soy sauce, sugar,
salt and garlic and stir-fry for 3-4 minutes
longer or until chicken is cooked.
Sprinkle with spring onions and coriander
and serve immediately.

*Serves 4*

When handling fresh chillies
do not put your hands near
your eyes or allow them to
touch your lips. To avoid
discomfort and burning,
wear rubber gloves. Freshly
minced chilli is available in
jars from supermarkets.

# CHICKEN AND CAULIFLOWER STIR-FRY

*Opposite: Chicken and Cauliflower Stir-fry, Sesame and Soy Chicken*

1$^{1}/_{4}$ teaspoons salt
$^{1}/_{2}$ teaspoon cornflour
1 teaspoon light soy sauce
$^{1}/_{4}$ teaspoon sugar
$^{1}/_{2}$ teaspoon sesame oil
250 g/8 oz boneless chicken breast
fillets, sliced
$^{1}/_{4}$ cup/60 mL/2 fl oz vegetable oil
3 cloves garlic, thinly sliced
$^{1}/_{2}$ cauliflower, broken into small florets
2 tablespoons water
2 stalks celery, sliced diagonally
1 carrot, sliced
1 tomato, sliced
$^{1}/_{4}$ cup/60 mL/2 fl oz water blended with
$^{1}/_{4}$ teaspoon cornflour

1   Combine $^{1}/_{2}$ teaspoon salt, cornflour, $^{1}/_{2}$ teaspoon soy sauce, sugar and $^{1}/_{4}$ teaspoon sesame oil in a bowl. Add chicken, toss and set aside to marinate for 10-15 minutes.

2   Heat 2 tablespoons vegetable oil in a wok or frying pan over a medium heat, add chicken and garlic and stir-fry for 4-5 minutes. Remove chicken mixture from pan and set aside.

3   Add remaining vegetable oil, cauliflower, $^{1}/_{4}$ teaspoon salt and water to pan and stir-fry for 3-4 minutes or until cauliflower is tender. Add celery, carrot and tomato and return chicken to pan and stir-fry for 3-4 minutes longer or until carrot is tender.

4   Combine remaining salt, remaining soy sauce and remaining sesame oil with cornflour mixture. Push chicken and vegetables to one side and stir soy sauce mixture into pan. When mixture boils, push chicken and vegetables into sauce and toss to combine.

*Serves 4*

# SESAME AND SOY CHICKEN

1 tablespoon heavy soy sauce (kicap soya)
1$^{1}/_{2}$ teaspoons sesame oil
4 chicken thighs
1 teaspoon sugar
$^{1}/_{2}$ teaspoon salt
1 tablespoon light soy sauce
$^{1}/_{2}$ cup/125 mL/4 fl oz water
2 tablespoons vegetable oil
1 star anise
2 whole cloves
3 thin slices fresh ginger
2 cloves garlic, bruised
1 spring onion, cut into 2.5 cm/1 in
pieces
1 tomato, sliced
$^{1}/_{2}$ cucumber, sliced
315 g/10 oz canned sliced pineapple,
drained

*Serves 4*

Serve with rice or Chilli Soy Noodles (page 71) and chilli garlic sauce for dipping.

1   Combine heavy soy sauce (kicap soya) and $^{1}/_{2}$ teaspoon sesame oil, rub evenly over chicken thighs and set aside to marinate for 10-15 minutes. Place  sugar, salt, remaining sesame oil, light soy sauce and water in a bowl, mix to combine and set aside.

2   Heat vegetable oil in a wok or frying pan over a medium heat, add star anise, cloves, ginger and garlic and stir-fry for 1-2 minutes or until fragrant. Add chicken mixture to pan and stir-fry for 5 minutes. Stir soy sauce mixture and spring onion into pan, bring to simmering and simmer for 10 minutes or until chicken is cooked. Remove star anise, cloves, ginger and garlic. Serve garnished with tomato, cucumber and pineapple.

# VEGETARIAN

*The most delicious Western vegetarian cooking owes much to Chinese cooks who have been practicing the art for thousands of years. Tasty, colourful and nutritious, these recipes are sure to become popular favourites at your table.*

## VEGETABLE AND TOFU CURRY

¹/4 cup/60 mL/2 fl oz vegetable oil
1 onion, finely chopped
6 cloves garlic, crushed
2 teaspoons ground ginger
2 teaspoons chilli powder
¹/4 teaspoon saffron powder
2¹/2 cups/600 mL/1 pt coconut milk
3 cups/750 mL/1¹/4 pt water
2 large cabbage leaves, shredded
4 tofu puffs, cut into thirds, or
250 g/8 oz pressed (firm) tofu, cut into
squares, deep fried
125 g/4 oz green beans, cut into
5 cm/2 in lengths
1¹/2 teaspoons salt
¹/4 teaspoon sugar

1   Heat oil in a wok or large frying pan over a medium heat, add onion, garlic, ginger and chilli powder and stir-fry for 2-3 minutes or until fragrant. Stir in saffron, coconut milk and water, bring to simmering.

2   Add cabbage, tofu puffs, beans, salt and sugar and simmer for 10-15 minutes or until vegetables are tender.

*Serves 4*

Serve this tasty curry on a bed of boiled white rice or noodles.
Tofu puffs are squares of deep-fried tofu. They are available in packets from Oriental food stores.

*Steamed Vegetarian Buns,
Vegetable and Tofu Curry*

# STEAMED VEGETARIAN BUNS

4 dried Chinese mushrooms
1 tablespoon vegetable oil
2 cloves garlic, crushed
30 g/1 oz button mushrooms, diced
1 small carrot, diced
60 g/2 oz tofu, diced
30 g/1 oz fresh or frozen peas
1 tablespoon oyster sauce
$^1/_2$ teaspoon sugar
$^1/_2$ teaspoon freshly ground black pepper
$^1/_4$ teaspoon salt
12 x 5 cm/2 in square pieces baking
paper

BUN DOUGH
$1^1/_2$ cups/185 g/6 oz self-raising flour
$^1/_2$ teaspoon baking powder
$^1/_4$ cup/60 g/2 oz sugar
pinch salt
$^1/_2$ cup/125 mL/4 fl oz water
1 tablespoon vegetable oil
1 teaspoon vinegar

1   Place Chinese mushrooms in a bowl, cover with boiling water and set aside to soak for 10 minutes or until mushrooms are tender. Drain, remove stalks if necessary and chop mushrooms.

2   Heat oil in a wok or frying pan over a medium heat, add Chinese mushrooms, garlic, button mushrooms, carrot and tofu and stir-fry for 4-5 minutes or until vegetables are almost cooked. Add peas, oyster sauce, sugar, black pepper and salt and stir-fry for 2-3 minutes longer or until heated through. Remove pan from heat and set aside to cool completely.

3   To make dough, sift flour and baking powder together into a large bowl, add sugar and salt and mix to combine. Add water, oil and vinegar and mix to form a soft dough. Turn dough onto a lightly floured surface and knead for 5-10 minutes or until dough is smooth. Cover and set aside to rest for 15 minutes.

4   Divide dough into 12 portions and working on a lightly floured surface, roll each portion into a ball. Lightly flatten each ball of dough to make a 10 cm/4 in round. Place a spoonful of filling in the centre of each dough round and brush the edges with water. Draw pastry around mixture and pinch together to form a bun.

5   Place bun join side down on a piece of the baking paper and place in a bamboo steamer. Repeat with remaining dough rounds and filling to use all ingredients.

6   Cover steamer with lid, place over a saucepan of simmering water and steam for 15-20 minutes or until buns are cooked through.

*Makes 12*

Before using a bamboo steamer for the first time, wash it well then place it over a saucepan of simmering water and steam it empty for about 5 minutes.

*Chilli Vegetarian*

# CHILLI VEGETABLES

¹/₄ teaspoon sugar
¹/₂ teaspoon salt
¹/₂ teaspoon sesame oil
1 tablespoon yellow bean paste
¹/₂ cup/125 mL/4 fl oz water
¹/₄ cup/60 mL/2 fl oz vegetable oil
1 large eggplant (aubergine), cut into chunks
2 large mushrooms, quartered
2 large oyster mushrooms, sliced
2 cm/³/₄ in piece fresh ginger, minced
2 cloves garlic, crushed
2 fresh red chillies, finely chopped
30 g/1 oz fresh or frozen peas

1   Place sugar, salt, sesame oil, bean paste and water in a small bowl, mix to combine and set aside.

2   Heat 2 tablespoons vegetable oil in a wok or frying pan over a medium heat, add eggplant (aubergine) and cook, turning frequently, until it begins to soften. Remove eggplant (aubergine) from pan and set aside.

3   Heat remaining vegetable oil in pan, add mushrooms, oyster mushrooms, ginger, garlic and chillies and stir-fry for 2-3 minutes or until fragrant.

4   Add bean paste mixture to pan and toss to coat all ingredients. Add eggplant (aubergine) and peas to pan and stir-fry for 2-3 minutes or until heated through.

*Serves 4*

To clean a wok, wash with water (do not use detergent), then dry thoroughly. The best way to dry the wok is to place it over a low heat for a few minutes.

# TOMATO AND CHILLI OMELETTE

Fresh chillies come in a variety of shapes and sizes and will keep in an airtight container in the refrigerator for 7-10 days. As a general rule the smaller, narrower and darker the chilli, the greater its potency.

2 eggs
$^1/_4$ teaspoon salt
$^1/_2$ tomato, finely chopped
$^1/_2$ onion, finely chopped
$^1/_2$ fresh red chilli, seeded and finely chopped
$^1/_2$ fresh green chilli, seeded and finely chopped
1 tablespoon vegetable oil

Place eggs and salt in a bowl and whisk to combine. Add tomato, onion and chillies and mix to combine. Heat oil in a small nonstick frying pan over a medium heat, add egg mixture and swirl to coat pan. Cook until omelette just begins to firm. Fold omelette in half, then in half again. Slide onto serving plate and serve immediately.

*Serves 1*

# EGG AND TOFU FRIED RICE

2¹/₂ tablespoons vegetable oil
125 g/4 oz tofu, diced
3 eggs, lightly beaten
1¹/₂ cups/330 g/10¹/₂ oz long grain rice,
cooked and cooled
60 g/2 oz green beans, chopped
¹/₄ teaspoon salt
¹/₄ teaspoon freshly ground black pepper
2 teaspoons light soy sauce

1   Heat 1 tablespoon oil in a wok or frying pan over a medium heat, add tofu and stir-fry for 2-3 minutes or until golden. Remove tofu from pan. Set aside.

2   Heat ¹/₂ tablespoon oil in pan. Pour eggs into pan, swirl to coat pan evenly and cook over a low heat until omelette is just set. Chop and set aside.

3   Add remaining oil and rice to pan and stir-fry for 3-4 minutes to separate grains. Add beans, salt, black pepper and soy sauce to pan and stir-fry for 3-4 minutes until beans are just cooked. Return tofu and omelette strips to pan and toss to combine.

One of the easiest ways to cook rice for fried rice is to cook it in the microwave. To cook rice in the microwave place 1 cup/220 g/7 oz rice and 2 cups/500 mL/16 fl oz water in a large microwave-safe container. Cook uncovered on HIGH (100%) for 12-15 minutes or until liquid is absorbed. Cover and stand for 5 minutes. Toss with a fork and use as required. Rice for fried rice should be completely cold before using – it is best to cook the rice the day before, then to chill it overnight.

*Left: Tomato and Chilli Omelette*
*Above: Egg and Tofu Fried Rice*

**Serves 2**

# SIDE DISHES

*Whether fried or steamed, noodles and rice are an essential addition to a Chinese meal. Apart from being important staples in China, they allow you to make the most of sauces and marinades right down to the last tasty drops.*

## GARLIC NOODLES WITH SEAFOOD

125 g/4 oz medium uncooked prawns,
shelled and deveined
1$^1$/$_4$ teaspoons sugar
salt
freshly ground black pepper
500 g/1 lb fresh round egg noodles
$^1$/$_3$ cup/90 mL/3 fl oz vegetable oil
2 tablespoons oyster sauce
4 cloves garlic, finely chopped
125 g/4 oz scallops
60 g/2 oz calamari (squid) rings
5 stalks mustard greens (choy sum)
$^1$/$_2$ teaspoon sesame oil
$^1$/$_2$ teaspoon light soy sauce
$^1$/$_2$ cup/125 mL/4 fl oz water blended
with 1 teaspoon cornflour and
1 teaspoon chicken stock powder
2 tablespoons chopped fresh coriander

1  Combine prawns, $^1$/$_4$ teaspoon sugar and salt and black pepper to taste in a bowl and marinate for 10-15 minutes.

2  Cook noodles in boiling water in a large saucepan, following packet directions. Drain well and rinse under cold running water. Allow noodles to drain in a colander.

3  Heat 2 tablespoons vegetable oil in a wok or frying pan over a medium heat, add noodles, oyster sauce, half the garlic and $^1$/$_2$ teaspoon sugar and stir-fry for 3-4 minutes or until garlic is golden. Remove from pan, set aside and keep warm.

4  Heat remaining vegetable oil in pan, add prawns, scallops, calamari, (squid), mustard greens (choy sum) and remaining garlic and stir-fry for 5 minutes or until seafood is almost cooked. Stir in remaining sugar, sesame oil, soy sauce, $^1$/$_4$ teaspoon salt, $^1$/$_4$ teaspoon black pepper and cornflour mixture and bring to the boil. To serve, place noodles on a serving platter, top with seafood mixture and sprinkle with coriander.

This dish is delicious accompanied by sliced red chillies or pickled green chillies and looks great garnished with coriander, fried onions and black pepper.

*Serves 2-4*

*Fragrant Steamed Rice,
Garlic Noodles with Seafood*

# FRAGRANT STEAMED RICE

$^1/_2$ teaspoon sugar
1 teaspoon salt
$^1/_2$ teaspoon freshly ground black pepper
$^1/_2$ teaspoon sesame oil
$1^1/_2$ tablespoons light soy sauce
2 tablespoons vegetable oil
185 g/6 oz lean pork mince
5 dried Chinese mushrooms
45 g/$1^1/_2$ oz dried shrimps
1 clove garlic, crushed
6 stalks bok choy, chopped (optional)
$1^1/_2$ cups/330 g/$10^1/_2$ oz long grain rice,
washed and drained
2 cups/500 mL/16 fl oz water

1   Place sugar, $^1/_2$ teaspoon salt, black pepper, sesame oil, soy sauce and 1 tablespoon vegetable oil in a bowl and mix to combine. Add pork, mix to combine and set aside to marinate for 10-15 minutes.

2   Place mushrooms in a bowl, cover with boiling water and set aside to soak for 10 minutes or until mushrooms are tender. Drain, remove stalks if neccessary and chop.

3   Remove any pieces of shell from shrimps. Place shrimps in a bowl, cover with hot water and set aside to soak for 10-15 minutes or until shrimps are tender. Drain and reserve soaking water.

4   Heat remaining vegetable oil in a wok or frying pan over a medium heat, add shrimps and stir-fry for 1-2 minutes or until fragrant. Add pork mixture, garlic, mushrooms, bok choy, if using, reserved shrimp soaking water, rice and remaining salt and stir-fry for 3-4 minutes.

5   Transfer mixture to a large saucepan, stir in water and bring to the boil. Reduce heat to low, cover and cook for 15-20 minutes or until liquid is absorbed and rice is tender.

*Serves 2*

Spinach or silverbeet can be used instead of bok choy.

*Special Fried Rice*

# SPECIAL FRIED RICE

4 tablespoons vegetable oil
2 eggs, lightly beaten with
$^1/_4$ teaspoon salt
45 g/1$^1/_2$ oz Chinese sausage (Lap Cheong), cut into 1 cm/$^1/_2$ in pieces
125 g/4 oz small uncooked prawns, shelled and deveined
500 g/1 lb rice, cooked and cooled
1$^1/_2$ tablespoons light soy sauce
$^1/_2$ teaspoon salt
125 g/4 oz Chinese barbecued pork or Chinese roast pork
2 spring onions, chopped

1   Heat 1 tablespoon oil in wok or frying pan over a low heat, pour egg mixture into pan, swirl to coat pan evenly and cook for 2-3 minutes or until omelette is set. As omelette cooks cut it into pieces using a spatula. Remove from pan and set aside.

2   Heat pan over a low heat, add sausage and stir-fry for 4-5 minutes or until crisp. Remove sausage from pan and set aside. Add 1 tablespoon oil and prawns to pan and stir-fry for 2 minutes or until they just change colour. Remove prawns from pan and set aside.

3   Heat remaining oil in pan, add rice and stir-fry for 3-4 minutes to separate grains. Add soy sauce and salt and stir-fry for 1-2 minutes. Add pork and return omelette, sausage and prawns to pan and stir-fry for 3-4 minutes or until heated through. Remove pan from heat, add spring onions and toss to combine.

*Serves 4*

Chinese sausages are highly flavoured sausages made with chopped lean and fatty pork and spices. They are available from Oriental food stores. Serve fried rice with sliced pickled green chillies.

# FRIED NOODLES WITH PORK

250 g/8 oz rice noodles (vermicelli)
light soy sauce
1 teaspoon salt
$^1/_2$ teaspoon sugar
1 teaspoon sesame oil
$^1/_4$ teaspoon freshly ground black pepper
$^1/_4$ teaspoon cornflour
125 g/4 oz pork belly or meat of your
choice, cut into 3 cm/$1^1/_4$ in strips
vegetable oil
2 eggs, lightly beaten
2 teaspoons oyster sauce
60 g/2 oz small uncooked prawns,
shelled and deveined
$^1/_2$ carrot, cut into 3 cm/$1^1/_4$ in strips
8 fresh chives, cut into
2.5 cm/1 in pieces
1 clove garlic, crushed
125 g/4 oz fish cake, cut into
3 cm/$1^1/_4$ in strips (optional)

1 Cook noodles in boiling water in a large saucepan following packet directions. Drain and set aside.

2 Place $1^1/_4$ teaspoons soy sauce, $^1/_4$ teaspoon salt, sugar, $^1/_2$ teaspoon sesame oil, black pepper and cornflour in a bowl and mix to combine. Add pork, toss to combine and set aside to marinate for 10-15 minutes.

3 Heat 1 tablespoon vegetable oil in wok or frying pan over a medium heat, pour eggs into pan, swirl to coat pan evenly and cook for 2-3 minutes or until omelette is set and golden on the base. Turn omelette onto a board, roll up, cut into strips and set aside.

4 Place 1 tablespoon soy sauce, remaining sesame oil, remaining salt and oyster sauce in a small bowl and mix to combine. Set aside.

5 Heat 1 tablespoon vegetable oil in pan over a medium heat, add pork and stir-fry for 4-5 minutes or until pork changes colour. Remove pork from pan and set aside.

6 Heat 1 tablespoon vegetable oil in pan over a medium heat, add prawns and stir-fry for 2 minutes or until prawns just change colour. Remove prawns from pan and set aside.

7 Heat $1^1/_4$ tablespoons vegetable oil in pan, add noodles, carrot, chives and garlic to pan and stir-fry for 2-3 minutes. Add oyster sauce mixture, fish cake, if using, omelette, pork and prawns to pan and stir-fry for 2-3 minutes or until heated through.

*Serves 4*

This dish looks great garnished with fried onions and sliced fresh red chillies. Fish cakes as used in this recipe are available from Oriental food stores.

# CHILLI SOY NOODLES

*Chilli Soy Noodles, Fried Noodles with Pork*

2$^1/_2$ tablespoons ginger oil
1$^1/_2$ tablespoons oyster sauce
1 tablespoon chilli sauce
1 teaspoon light soy sauce
$^1/_4$ teaspoon sesame oil
3 x 75 g/2$^1/_2$ oz cakes instant noodles

1   Place ginger oil, oyster sauce, chilli sauce, soy sauce and sesame oil in a bowl and mix to combine. Set aside.

2   Prepare noodles following packet directions. Drain well. Add sauce to noodles and toss to combine. Serve immediately.

*Serves 2*

To make ginger oil refer to glossary (page 78). Garnish these noodles with chopped spring onions if desired.

# DESSERTS

*What better way to conclude your Chinese menu
and impress guests and family than with one of these
special desserts. These recipes, including Pandan Chiffon
Cake and Fruit Salad with Almond Jelly, taste every
bit as good as they sound.*

## STEAMED BANANA CAKE

2 ripe bananas
60 g/2 oz green mung pea flour (tepung
hun kwe) or arrowroot
$^1/_2$ cup/125 g/4 oz sugar
pinch salt
$2^1/_4$ cups/560 mL/18 fl oz coconut milk
$^3/_4$ cup/185 mL/6 fl oz water
red food colouring

1   Place bananas with skins on in steamer, set over a saucepan of simmering water and steam for 5-8 minutes or until bananas are soft. Remove from steamer and set aside to cool. Peel bananas, dice and set aside.

2   Place flour or arrowroot, sugar and salt in a bowl and mix to combine. Combine coconut milk and water and slowly stir into flour. Strain mixture into a saucepan and cook, stirring constantly, over a medium heat for 8-10 minutes or until mixture boils and thickens.

3   Remove pan from heat and pour half the mixture into a 15 x 23 cm/6 x 9 in glass or ceramic dish rinsed in cold water. Top with bananas. Colour remaining coconut milk mixture with food colouring. Spoon over bananas, set aside to cool and set. To serve, cut into diamond shapes.

*Makes 50*

Green mung pea flour often labelled as tepung hun kwe is available from Oriental food stores. If it is unavailable arrowroot is a suitable substitute however the flavour will be a little different.

*Fruit Salad with Almond Jelly,
Steamed Banana Cake*

# FRUIT SALAD WITH ALMOND JELLY

2$^1$/2 teaspoons agar agar powder
$^1$/4 cup/60 g/2 oz caster sugar
2 cups/500 mL/16 fl oz water
$^1$/2 teaspoon almond essence
75 mL/2$^1$/2 fl oz evaporated milk
440 g/14 oz canned fruit salad
440 g/14 oz canned longans or lychees
or a selection of fresh fruit

1   Place agar agar powder, sugar and a
little water in a bowl and mix to dissolve
agar agar. Place remaining water in a
saucepan and bring to the boil over a
medium heat. Lower heat, stir in agar
agar mixture and cook, stirring
constantly, for 5 minutes.

2   Remove pan from heat, stir in almond
essence and evaporated milk and mix
well to combine. Pour mixture into a
shallow 20 cm/8 in square cake tin and
refrigerate until set. To serve, place fruit
salad and longans or lychees with juice
in a large bowl. Cut jelly into bite-sized
wedges or cubes and add to fruit mixture.
Chill until ready to serve.

*Serves 10-12*

Agar agar is an extract of
seaweed and is used by
vegetarians instead of
gelatine.

# PANDAN CHIFFON CAKE

Oven temperature
180°C, 350°F, Gas 4

$^1$/2 cup/60 g/2 oz flour
3 teaspoons baking powder
6 eggs, separated
$^1$/2 teaspoon cream of tartar
1$^1$/4 cups/280 g/9 oz caster sugar
$^1$/4 cup/60 mL/2 fl oz vegetable oil
$^3$/4 cup/185 mL/6 fl oz coconut milk
1 teaspoon pandan essence

1   Sift together flour and baking powder
three times and set aside.

2   Place egg whites and cream of tartar in
a bowl, beat until stiff peaks form. Set
aside.

3   Place egg yolks and sugar in a bowl
and beat until light and fluffy. Stir in oil,
coconut milk and pandan essence. Fold in
flour mixture and mix well to combine.
Using a metal spoon, fold egg white
mixture into egg yolk mixture in batches.

4   Spoon batter into an ungreased
23 cm/9 in ring tin and bake for 45
minutes. Stand cake in tin for 5 minutes
before turning onto a wire rack to cool.

*Serves 8*

Pandan essence is made
from the leaves of the
pandanus or screw pine and
is used as a flavouring and
colouring in Asian and Indian
cooking. It is pale-green in
colour with a warm nutlike
flavour and is available from
Oriental food stores. For more
information on pandan
essence see glossary (page
78).

*Pandan Chiffon Cake*

# GLOSSARY

**Agar agar:** This is an extract of seaweed and is used in Asian cooking as a substitute for gelatine. It comes in either small transparent strips of various colours or powder form. When dissolved in water over a low heat, agar agar blends with water and on cooling sets to a jelly. It is very important that agar agar is completely dissolved before cooking. Stir in boiling water and simmer over a low heat for 5 minutes. It will set in about an hour at room temperature. To set 1 cup/250 mL/8 fl oz of liquid you will require 8 g/$^1$/$_4$ oz agar agar. It should be noted that dishes that use agar agar do not require refrigeration to remain firm and set.

**Bean curd sheets:** Available from Oriental food stores and some health food shops and supermarkets, this is the skin that forms during the making of tofu (bean curd). It is skimmed off the boiled mixture then dried. It is sometimes called bean curd skin.

**Bean sauces and pastes:** There are a huge range of bean sauces and pastes available in Oriental food stores. These include yellow and black bean sauce, black bean garlic sauce and chilli bean sauce. Most are made from puréed soy beans with various seasonings added.

**Candlenut:** Also known as kermiri in Indonesia and buah keras in Malaysia, these are the nuts of the candleberry tree. They are an oily nut with a very hard shell, very similar to macadamia nuts. Macadamia nuts are the perfect substitute if candlenuts are unavailable. Raw cashews or brazil nuts are also suitable substitutes. Candlenuts are available from Oriental food stores.

**Chinese barbecued pork or Chinese roast pork (char siew):** Available from Oriental food stores that sell meat. Pork fillet is marinated in a soy sauce mixture then roasted at a high temperature. The result is a red coloured pork with a crusty surface. If unavailable roast pork can be used instead.

**Chinese sausage (lap cheong):** These are highly flavoured sausages made with chopped lean and fatty pork and spices. They are available from Oriental food stores. If unavailable any spicy sausage can be substituted.

**Cloud ears:** These black fungi, also known as wood ears, are available from Oriental food stores. Like dried Chinese mushrooms they have to be soaked in hot water until soft before using. If unavailable dried Chinese mushrooms can be used instead.

**Coconut milk:** This can be purchased in a number of forms – canned, as a long-life product in cartons or as a powder to which you add water. Once opened it has a short life and should be used with a day or so.

You can make coconut milk using desiccated coconut and water. To make coconut milk, place 500 g/1 lb desiccated coconut in a bowl and pour over 3 cups/750 mL/1$^1$/$_4$ pt boiling water. Leave to stand for 30 minutes, then strain, squeezing the coconut to extract as much liquid as possible. This will make a thick coconut milk. The coconut can be used again to make a weaker milk.

**Coriander:** Also known as Chinese parsley or cilantro, this is an attractive annual which grows to 60 cm/2 ft. The lacy foliage has a distinctive, strong aroma. It is a popular in many Asian cuisines.

**Dried chestnuts:** Available from Oriental food stores these should not be confused with water chestnuts. Before using soak dried chestnuts in hot water until soft – this will take about 30 minutes. Then using the tip of a sharp knife carefully remove the skin.

**Dried Chinese mushrooms:** These are fairly expensive, but a few will add a unique flavour to any dish. To use dried mushrooms, place mushrooms in a bowl, cover with boiling water and set aside to soak for 10 minutes or until soft. Squeeze out excess liquid, remove tough stem and use as required. For added flavour, the soaking liquid is often added to dishes.

**Fish sauce:** This is the drained liquid from salted fermented anchovies.

*Clockwise from top left: Choy sum, lemon grass, coriander, bok choy, tofu puffs, Chinese fried bread, saffron threads, saffron powder, black fungi, shrimp powder, pandan essence, fish cake, bamboo shoots (sliced and whole), selection Oriental noodles, tamarind pulp, baby sweet corn, straw mushrooms, fortune cookies, water chestnuts, red bean curd, dried chillies, red and green chillies, firm tofu, soft tofu, spring roll wrappers, dried chestnuts, dried bean curd sheets, dried Chinese mushrooms, candlenuts, ginger, garlic, star anise, lychees*

**Ginger juice:** This is simply the juice extracted from fresh ginger. If a large quantity is required use a juicer to extract the juice. For small quantities the easiest way to extract the juice is by using a garlic crusher.

**Ginger oil:** This is easy to make yourself and adds a delicious flavour to any dish it is used in. Use for frying fish, in soups, when marinating meat, added to cooked vegetables and in steamed dishes. To make ginger oil, place 4 cups/1 litre/1³/₄ pt vegetable oil and a 1 cm/¹/₂ in piece of peeled fresh ginger in a large saucepan and bring to simmering over a medium heat. Remove pan from heat and set aside to cool. Strain and store in a bottle. This makes 4 cups/1 litre/1³/₄ pt ginger oil.

**Green mung pea flour:** Often labelled as tepung hun kwe this is available from Oriental food stores. It is made from the tiny green peas which are sprouted to form bean sprouts. When looking for this product it is worth noting that green pea flour will often be stamped across the packet. If unavailable arrowroot is a suitable substitute however the flavour will be a little different.

**Hoisin sauce:** Also known as Chinese barbecue sauce, this is a thick, dark brown sauce made from soy beans, vinegar, sugar, spices and other flavourings. It has a sweet spicy flavour and is mainly used in southern Chinese cooking.

**Kechap manis:** This is a thick sweet seasoning sauce used in Asian cooking. It is made of soy sauce, sugar and spices. If unavailable soy sauce or a mixture of soy sauce and dark corn syrup or golden syrup can be used in its place.

**Lemon grass:** Fresh lemon grass is available from Oriental food stores and some supermarkets and green grocers. It is also available dried; if using dried lemon grass soak it in hot water for 20 minutes or until soft. Lemon grass is also available in bottles from supermarkets, use this in the same way as you would fresh lemon grass. There is also a powdered form available which is called sereh, this is strong in flavour and should be used with discretion. If lemon grass is unavailable lemon balm, lemon verbena or lemon rind are possible substitutes.

**Longan:** These are the fruit of the soapberry tree. They are similar to lychees, but are not as fragrant. Like lychees they are available canned from Oriental food stores. The Chinese call them 'dragon's eyes'.

**Red bean curd:** This is pressed bean curd which has been fermented with rice wine, salt, spices and red rice. It has a pungent flavour and is available in jars or cans from Oriental food stores.

**Pandan essence:** Made from the leaves of the pandanus or screw pine, this essence is used as a flavouring and colouring in Asian and Indian cooking. It is pale-green in colour and has a warm nutlike flavour. It is available as a powder or a liquid. Vanilla essence can be used in its place but the colour and flavour of the dish will be different. Food flavoured with pandan essence has a distinctive green colour. If you wish to retain this colour and pandan essence is unavailable, vanilla essence and green food colouring can be used instead.

**Plum sauce:** A popular dipping sauce, plum sauce is made from plums preserved in vinegar, sugar, chillies and spices.

**Saffron:** Saffron is the most expensive spice in the world. It is the dried stigmas of the flowers of the saffron crocus. The stigmas are extracted from the freshly harvested flowers and dried to become irregular, orange-red threads about 4 cm/1¹/₂ in long. It takes about 50,000 stigmas to make 100 g/3¹/₂ oz saffron. Saffron imparts a distinctive aroma, a bitter honey-like taste and a strong yellow colour to food. It is better to buy the threads and they should be stored in an airtight container in a dark place. Ground saffron can vary enormously in quality.

**Sesame seed oil:** This strongly flavoured oil is used as a seasoning and is made from roasted sesame seeds. Usually added at the end of cooking, it is available from Oriental food stores and keeps indefinitely.

**Shrimp powder:** This pungent ingredient is available from Oriental food stores and some supermarkets. It is made by pounding dried salted shrimp to a powder. Do not be put off by the odour as this disappears when cooked with other ingredients.

**Soy sauce:** In this book three types of soy sauce are used: light, dark and heavy. The Chinese use light soy sauce for cooking. In Chinese food stores it is labelled Superior Soy. Dark soy sauce is aged for longer than the light one, is slightly thicker and has a stronger flavour. The Chinese prefer to use this sauce as a dipping sauce and in stews. In Chinese food stores it is labelled Soy Superior Sauce. Heavy soy sauce, labelled as kicap soya, has a thick treacle-like consistency and is used more for colour than flavour. It is used in Asian cooking in the same way as Western cooks would use gravy browning – to enhance the colour of a dish. If unavailable gravy browning is the perfect substitute.

**Star anise:** This is the star-shaped fruit of an Oriental evergreen of the magnolia family. When dried it is a brown colour and the flavour is one of pungent aniseed. Whole stars store well in an airtight container and are available from Oriental food stores.

**Tamarind:** This is the large pod of the tamarind or Indian date tree. After picking, it is seeded and peeled then pressed into a dark brown pulp. To use, dilute the pulp with water then strain and use as directed in the recipe. The usual dilution is three parts water to one part tamarind. There is also a tamarind concentrate or paste available. If using this it should be diluted with double the amount of water that you would use when diluting the pulp. Tamarind is

available from Oriental and Indian food stores. If unavailable use a mixture of lime or lemon juice and treacle as a substitute. Use 1 part molasses to 3 parts lime or lemon juice, eg 1 tablespoon molasses to 3 tablespoons lime or lemon juice.

**Tofu:** Also known as bean curd, tofu has played an important role in Oriental cooking for over a thousand years. It is made from yellow soy beans which are soaked, ground and mixed with water then briefly cooked before being solidified. Rich in protein, it is low in fat and is cholesterol free. The range of bean curd products available in Oriental food stores is considerable and gives you an idea of how important this food is to the cuisines of the area.

**Tofu puffs:** Sometimes called fried bean curd, these are squares of deep-fried tofu. You will find them in packs in the refrigerator section of Oriental food stores. You can make your own tofu puffs at home by cutting pressed (firm) tofu into squares then deep-frying it.

**Water chestnuts:** White, crunchy and about the size of the walnut, water chestnuts are a sweet root vegetable. Canned water chestnuts are available from Oriental food stores and some supermarkets. In some Asian countries, fresh water chestnuts are boiled in their skins, then peeled and simmered with rock sugar and eaten as a snack. When using canned water chestnuts rinse them well first.

# INDEX